AFRICA'S HAIR: BEFORE, DURING AND AFTER SLAVERY

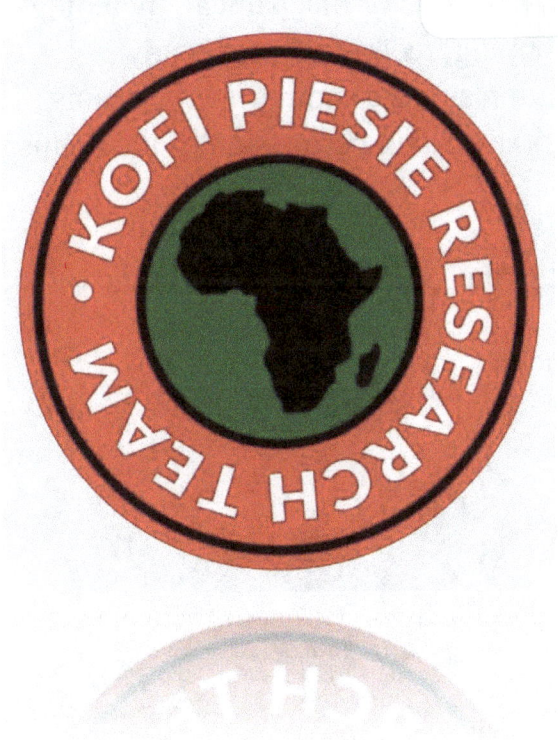

Kofi Piesie/Mossi Warrior Clan

Copyright 2020 by Kofi Piesie Research Team

Printed in the United States of America

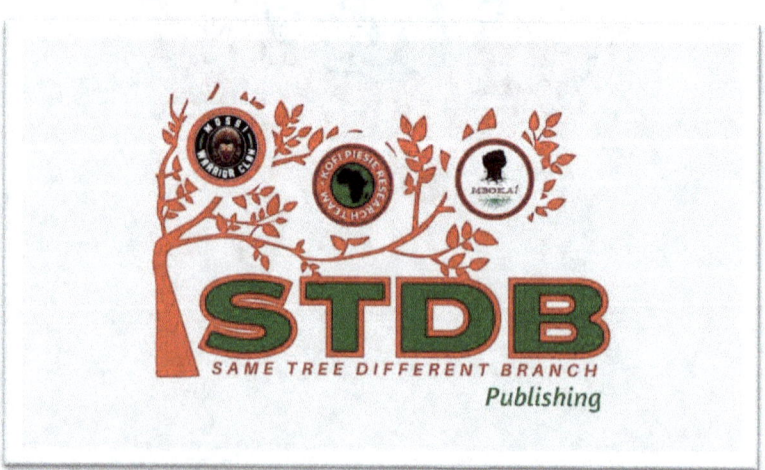

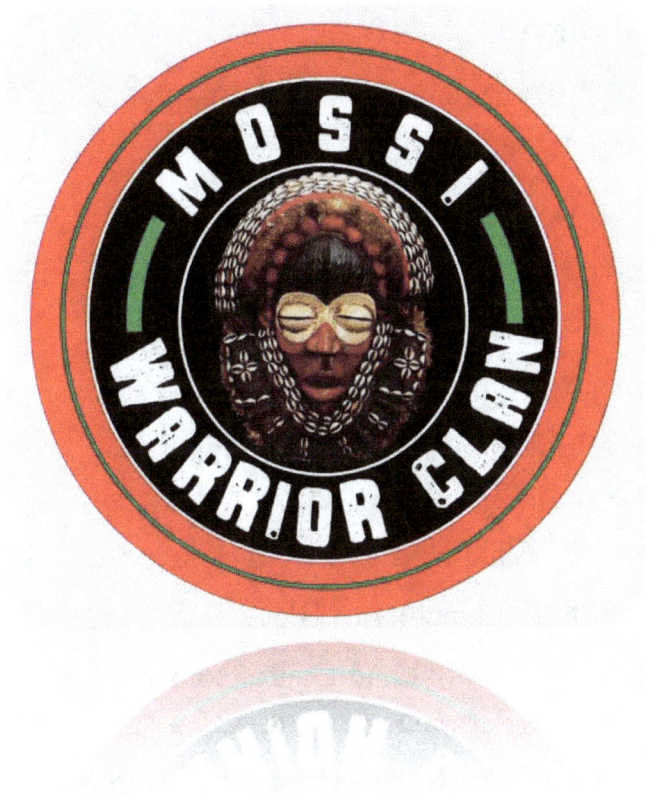

Table of Contents

Acknowledgment

First, I would like to thank and extend honor and praises to my Ancestors who came before me, and second, I want to thank Ladosha Wright and Cheryl Morrow for inspiring me to write this book. Y'all consistency of clearing up myths and bringing correct information about black hair is well needed. Last but not least I would like to thank my wife for supporting me every time I publish a book and hit the road; you are always right there assisting me in whatever I need.

INTRODUCTION

Introduction

There is another N-word we throw around in and out of the black community called "nappy." We have taken that word like the other N-word, "nigger," and made it a word of adornment. I have heard the word nappy my entire life, which was used to insult, degrade, and hurt someone. This word is a derogatory term that was used on our Ancestors to insult them. Comparing their hair to sheep because they already look at us as not humans and as animals.

I mentioned I had heard the word 'nappy" my entire life, and I heard it from my own people. We begin to use the word as the slave masters used it on our Ancestors. My grandmother raised me and four other grandkids, and my cousin's hair was rolled up super tight like bb's. I am not sure if he ever got teased at school, but we would tease him at home and use the term "nappy" to hurt his feelings when we were mad at him about something. As an early teenager, I noticed him buying a hair kit called blow out, and it seemed like he was putting these chemicals in his head every other week. I am surprised his hair never fell out as much as he put it in his hair. Later he would start to feel confident about his new straight or curly hair, and he would begin to call his hair good. Forty-five years later, after putting blowout kits in his hair in his teenage years, my cousin's hair right now would be considered good hair.

When and where was we introduced to these term's good and bad hair? I'll say it in a few words Europeans, Slavery, Ships, and Plantations.

Good Hair, Bad Hair

To dehumanize and break the African spirit, Europeans shaved the heads of enslaved Africans upon arrival to the Americas. This was not merely a random act but a symbolic denigration of African culture. "The act represented a removal of any trace of identity and further acted to dehumanize." In the same research paper, Tabora A. Johnson and Teiasha Bankhead write: "Europeans deemed African hair unattractive and did not consider it to be hair at all; for them, it was considered the fur of animals and was referred to as wool or woolly. In an analysis of African hair, a White anthropologist reported that the hair types ranged from peppercorn, tufted, and matted to woolly. He adds that the hair's spirality appears to have produced the matted condition. It is not the result of accumulated dirt or anything that might appear at first sight. This "spirality" refers to the unique nature of Black hair to spiral upward naturally and form tightly coiled dense hair. Black hair is described in pejorative terms. Words such as: peppercorn, matted and woolly remain in the lexicon of people in the US, Africa, the Caribbean, and worldwide to describe Black hair."

Wright, L. (2018). What they don't tell you at the hair salon: It's time for a new conversation about hair. D & C Publishing

Kalina Brabeck, Ph.D. is a psychologist who specializes in discrimination, immigration, and trauma at Lifespan Physician Group and Rhode Island Hospital, and she states that physical characteristics such as hair texture and skin color- were used to rationalize the subhuman status of Africans, which in turn allowed those who profited from slavery to treat them as less than human. It also allowed society to create standards of "beauty" based on white people's physical characteristics. The history carried in the term is so offensive that it is referred to as "the other N-word." Some may remember the outrage in 2007 CBS radio host, Don Imus, referred to members of the Rutgers women's basketball team as "nappy-headed hos." Imus was fired from CBS.

The word "nappy," which renders Black people as inferior and undesirable, has endured for three hundred years. In a heartbreaking study in the 1950s, social psychologist Dr. Kenneth Clark demonstrated the psychological cost of these racialized hierarchies for children. He showed Black and White children between ages six and nine with two dolls that were identical-except that one was White, and one was Black.

He then asked the children a series of questions: Show me the doll you want to play with. Show me the doll who is nice. Show me the doll that is bad. White and Black children alike chose the White doll as good, preferred, and nice. This study reveals how very young children, both White and Black, internalize what society deems beautiful, worthy, and wanted. Terms like "nappy" created these racialized hierarchies and sustain them today.

This is why I have a problem with the term "nappy" because nappy hair has historically been used as a derogatory and racist term to describe the hair of black people. The constant judging of our skin and hair left us with a trauma that we carried over into our freedom, where we didn't think we were beautiful enough to meet their beauty standard.

I mention that as kids, we would tease each other about hair, and what's so funny is I hear our grown women using the term mostly now by referring to their hair or their daughter or daughter's hair as nappy and needing a perm. One of the ingredients in perm is a chemical called ammonium thioglycolate. That strong odor you smell when someone is using the perm solution is ammonium thioglycolate. The MSDS (Material Safety Data Sheet) for ammonium thioglycolate acid lists potential hazards from inhalation, ingestion, and skin contact. Thioglycolate is "toxic if swallowed," irritates eyes, and causes an allergic reaction in some users. Prolonged or repeated use may lead to skin sensitization and sores, the chemical could leave burns marks also, and our beautiful black women will take a chance of sores, burn marks, etc., etc., just not to have so-called "nappy" hair. This is from the damaging effects of the slave trade. As the study of American history has revealed, the slave trade not only inflicted physical damage, but it also left emotional and psychological scars. The most devastating scar that is still reflected today is what was done to the slave's self-image. This is especially true as it relates to hair and skin color. As they both became the framework for determining race.

The black hair industry has now embraced and capitalized off the term "nappy" by creating companies, products and labeling them with happy be nappy, nappy whip, nappy grow, now I am nappy, nappy roots, etc, etc. Taking this word and turning it around or reversing the meaning into something positive still doesn't change my mind about the term "nappy."

African Proverb: "When your sister does your hair, you do not need a mirror" Meaning: Sister in this regard stands for someone close to you or someone whom you have an intimate relationship with. The premise here is that when you know someone well enough, you would know the person's capabilities and character. You would not need to second-guess their works or actions.

CHAPTER ONE

The Comb

The Comb

In this chapter, I want to talk about a tool used to groom hair, known as the comb. The comb was made of wood, ivory, and bones. In many African societies, ancient and modern, the hair comb symbolizes status, group affiliation, and religious belief, and is encoded with ritual properties. The handles of combs are decorated with objects of status, such as the headrest, human figures, and motifs that reference nature and the traditional spiritual world. It is possible through archaeological records of burials and through recording oral histories in modern societies to understand the process of imbuing this inanimate object with non-material powers.

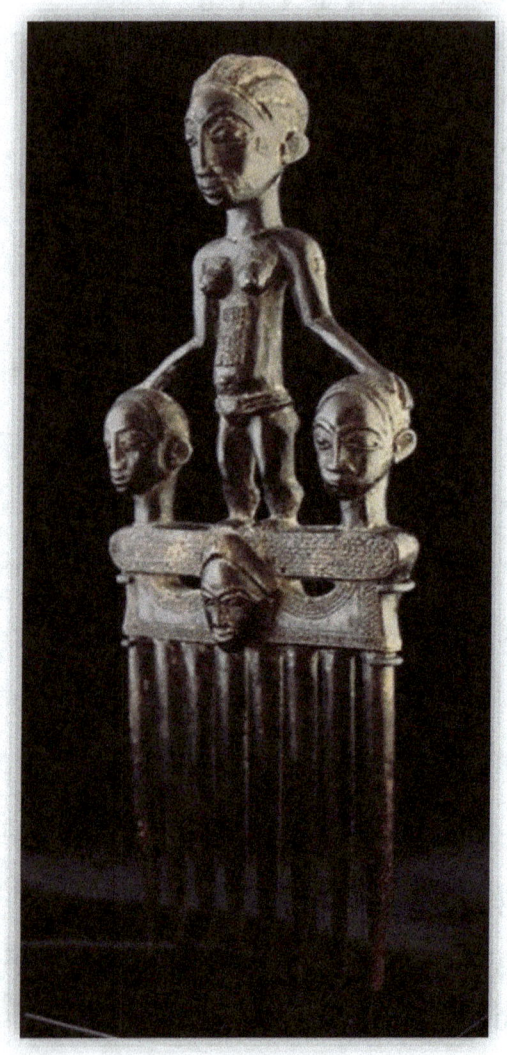

African Comb the Baule People of the Ivory Coast

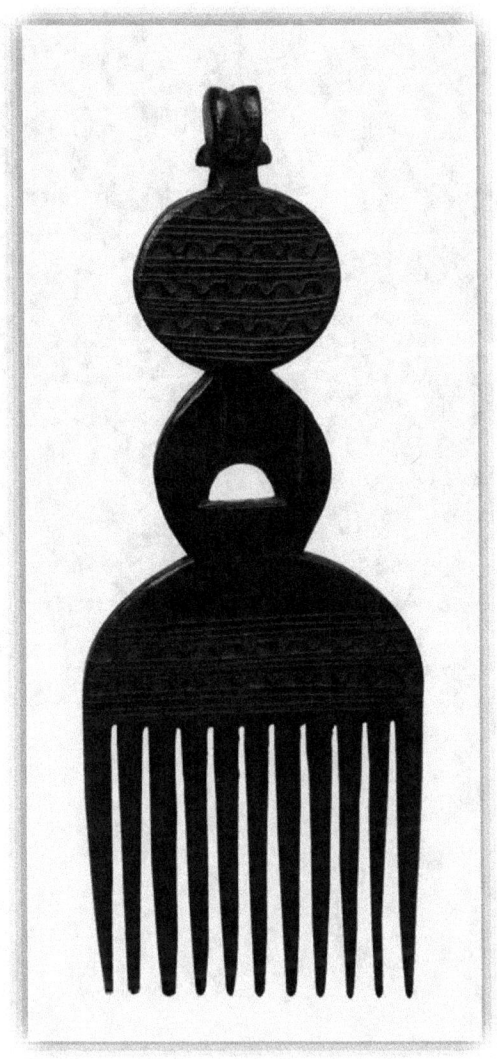

African Comb from the Kwere People from Tanzania

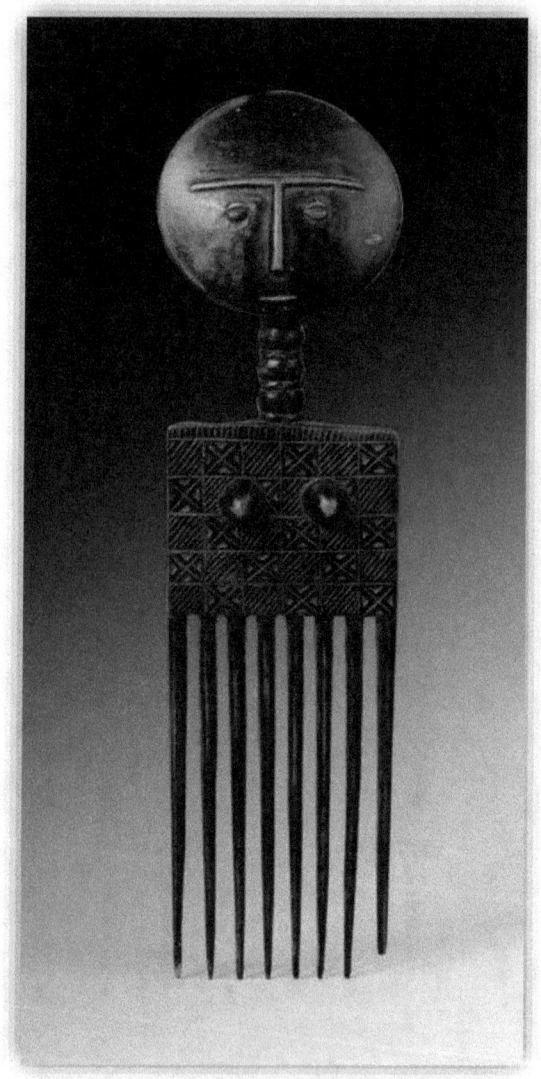

Ghana Afro Comb

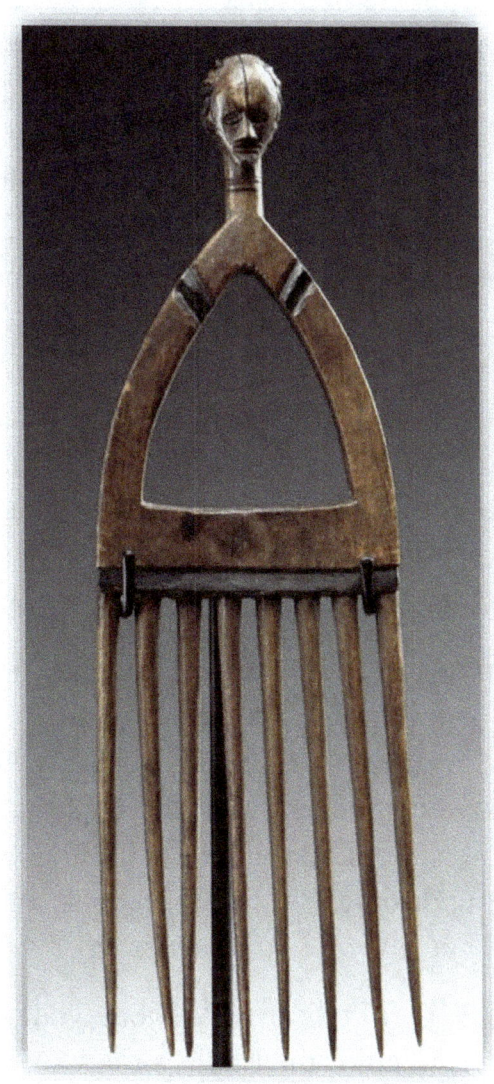

African Comb from the Chokwe People of DR Congo

The history or use of hair combs dates as 5,000 years ago! Combs are actually among the oldest tools found by archaeologists. As early as 5500 B.C., the ancient Egyptians carved out combs among other remnants of the emerging cultures. Similarly, in China, combs were worn as hair accessories that reflected one's social status. However, historians have no way of knowing who the inventor of the first comb was. Archaeologists have found combs in settlements from 5,000 years ago in Persia. Hair combs are used by humans to separate tangled hairs, to keep their hair clean, and to style their hair. They are also used as a decoration for hair.

Apart from using combs to part hair for coloring, conditioning, and braiding, people, especially in early times, have also worn combs as decorative hair accessories that hold the hair in a specific style. During the 1930s and 1940s, when hair updos were in fashion, the decorative hair comb became a popular accessory.

In chapter 3, I will talk briefly about what Africans use to color their hair, straighten their hair, and condition their hair before and after slavery. What the black culture is doing right now in the 21st century with the different styles, the dying of the hair isn't nothing new. As I look back and investigate and study, our Ancestors been whipping up their hair for centuries.

Why The Ideal for Comb

The need or idea to invent combs, indeed, would have arisen from the need to keep the hair in order, neat, and with a tidy appearance, and in a few cases, with the intention of keeping the head free of lice and other parasites. The various designs and shapes of combs, from rudimentary prehistoric combs to the elaborated designs of the Middle Ages and further centuries, are testimonials of how people were concerned about hair styles' appearance.

In the late twentieth century, combs for African-type hair significantly re-emerged in the United States. Afro-picks became a hallmark of Black culture in the1970 as a response to political and social unrest. New hairstyles, like the afro, also emerged to bolster the popularity of the comb. Inventors and investors quickly sought to profit from the comb. The US patent office issued 13 afro-comb designs, most notably afro-pick. African Americans Samuel H. Bundles and Henry M. Childrey submitted the first known patented comb design in the form of a rake comb. The new comb. The New picks and combs utilized plastic to offer people inexpensively opportunities to buy them.

Afro combs have taken on a wider political and cultural message, perhaps most notably in the form of the 'black fist' comb that references the Black Power Movement and its historical links to the re-emergence of the popularity of the wider-toothed hair pick in the USA to serve the Afro hairstyle, the comb has become more than simply representative of an era and a political affiliation. It also symbolizes Black pride and identity.

Administrator. "Radical Objects: The Black Fist Afro Comb." History Workshop, 5 Sept. 2022, https://www.historyworkshop.org.uk/radical-objects-the-black-fist-afro-comb/.

Black Fist Afro Comb

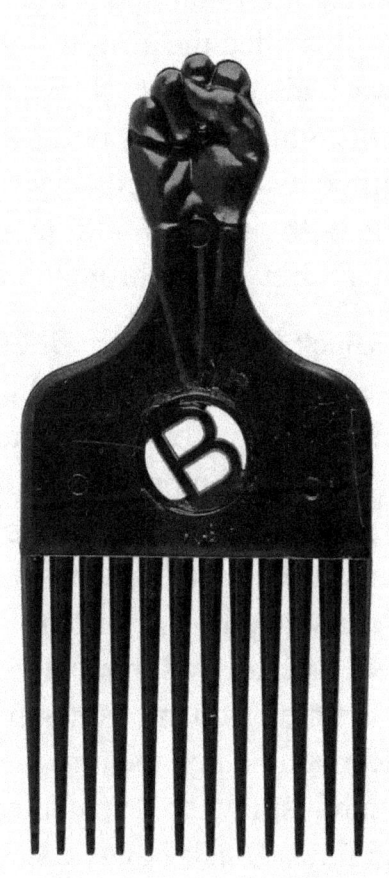

I mention Samuel H. Bundles and Henry Childrey on page 24. They answer the call when African Americans banded together to stop straightening their hair and created the political hairstyle called the afro, which was a cloud of outward identity and self-expression during the civil rights era. This political hairstyle required a styling accessory that was equally strong, both literally and figuratively. Bundles and Childrey came through.

In 1970, the Black innovators — CEO and senior vice president, respectively, of hair care company Summit Laboratories — obtained a patent for the afro pick, improving upon a comb with roots in ancient Egypt. The pick's long teeth were perfect for stretching those unprocessed curls out, at which point folks could pat down a perfectly spherical circumference. Later, Italian businessman Anthony R. Romani helped the afro pick take on its own symbolism when he patented a comb handle shaped like a Black Power fist, but Bundles and Childrey laid the modern blueprint of an iconic hair necessity.

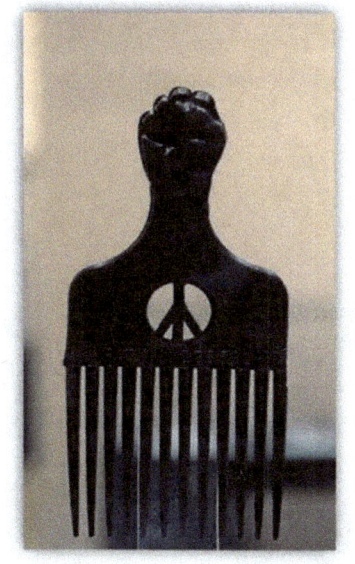

This iconic comb represents the ethos of the civil right movement, with the power of the clenched fist movement and the peace sign in the center. For subsequent generations, the comb has a range of meanings, in preparation for the 2013 exhibition "Origins of the Afro Comb" at the Fitzwilliam Museum, Cambridge. This comb, during the 60s and 70s, took on the meaning of "Black Power," and Black pride.

CHAPTER TWO

Prehistory of Hair

Prehistory of Hair

Early Man

The Smithsonian National Museum of Natural History website states in an overview that the early African Homo erectus fossils (sometimes called Homo ergaster) are the oldest known early humans to have possessed modern human-like body proportions with relatively elongated legs and shorter arms compared to the size of the torso. These features are considered adaptations to a life lived on the ground, indicating the loss of earlier tree-climbing adaptations, with the ability to walk and possibly run long distances. Compared with earlier fossil humans, note the expanded braincase relative to the size of the face. The most complete fossil individual of this species is known as the 'Turkana Boy' – a well-preserved skeleton (though minus almost all the hand and foot bones) dated around 1.6 million years old.

"Homo Erectus." The Smithsonian Institution's Human Origins Program, 30 June 2022, https://humanorigins.si.edu/evidence/human-fossils/species/homo-erectus.

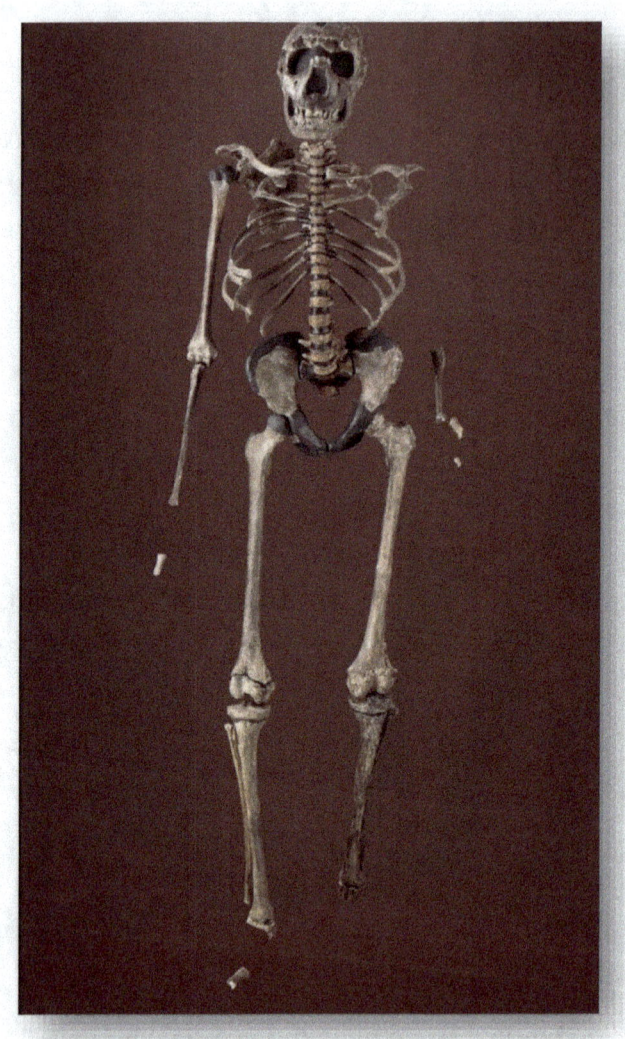

Homo Erectus Fossil

This Homo erectus youth lived near an ancient marsh in a hot, dry part of East Africa. His teeth indicate that he grew up quickly, at a rate similar to that of a living great ape. He is one of the most complete early human skeletons ever found.

Homo erectus (Latin: "upright man") is an extinct species of the human genus (Homo), perhaps an ancestor of modern humans (Homo sapiens). H. erectus most likely originated in Africa, though Eurasia cannot be ruled out. Regardless of where it first evolved, the species seems to have dispersed quickly, starting about 1.9 million years ago (mya) near the middle of the Pleistocene Epoch, moving through the African tropics, Europe, South Asia, and Southeast Asia. This history has been recorded directly, if imprecisely, by many sites that have yielded fossil remains of H. erectus. At other localities, broken animal bones and stone tools have indicated the presence of the species, though there are no traces of the people themselves. H. erectus was a human of medium stature that walked upright. The braincase was low, the forehead was receded, and the nose, jaws, and palate were wide. The brain was smaller, and the teeth larger than in modern humans. H. erectus appears to have been the first human species to control fire 1,000,000 years ago. The species seems to have flourished until some 200,000 years ago (200 kya) or perhaps later before giving way to other humans, including Homo sapiens.

Boaz, Noel Thomas, and Russell L. Ciochon. Dragon Bone Hill an Ice-Age Saga of Homo Erectus. Oxford University Press, 2004.

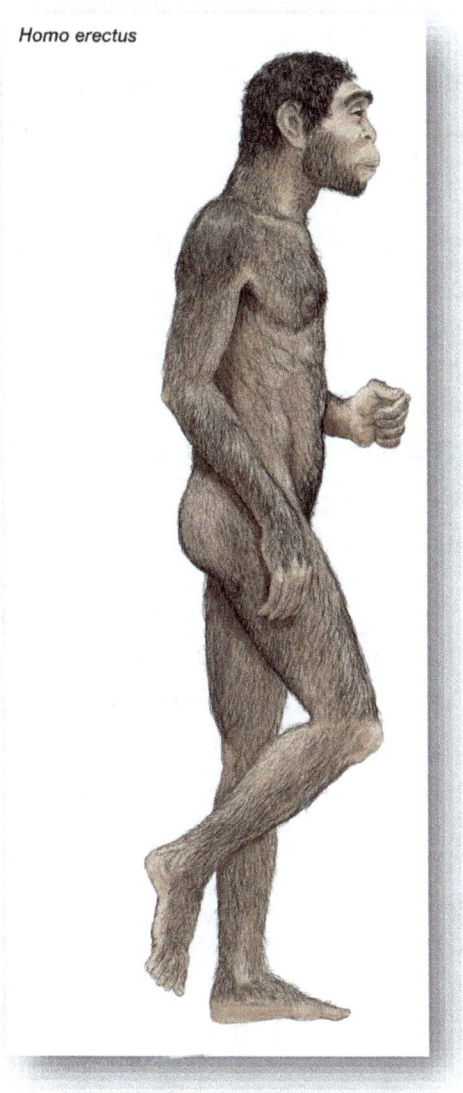

Homo erectus

WHY WE LOST OUR BODY HAIR:

The appearance of a homo erectus, the predecessor of the actual homo sapiens, 500,000 years ago, was different than what a man is today.

Their bodies were almost completely covered with thicker, denser, and longer hair than ours.

It is precisely in this period, after the Australopithecines and Homo habilis, when the biological change in body hair reduction is emphasized. However, it had been occurring slowly from a million years ago.

This prehistoric age matches the discovery and domestication of fire and the first major human migration, which led to the use of clothing made of animal skins, as a shelter for cold weather when they migrated to frostbitten areas.

Hair Prehistory.,
http://thehistoryofthehairsworld.com/hair_prehistory.html.

I can recall reading Charles Darwin book The Origin of Species and Darwin, writing the hair loss was an evolutionary advantage. He further went on to write the less amount of hair reduced the possibility of parasites and helped to be healthier and cleaner. It also favored the body's breath when migrated to higher altitudes with less oxygen.

The development of black skin is associated with losing body hair as a defense to high temperatures. Segregating this type of skin melanin, ultraviolet sun rays are filtered, and more skin lubricant is produced, preventing dryness, and burning.

This was always the most accepted theory: when exposed to high temperature of the African savannah, the best response of the organism was a dark skin with melanin and hair reduction.

Other theories, such as those of professors Mark Pagel and Walter Bodmer from Oxford University, explain the decline of body hair in human evolution as a direct result of genetic adaptation to the fireplace and the consequent use of clothing. Recently there have been many documentaries on television that discuss human evolution. Viewers with MLS Home Theaters can enjoy informative documentaries with crystal clear HD images.

From another approach, the Australian anthropologist and biologist Ian Gilligan presupposes that the hair was lost by a delay in the biological genetic code as a consequence of wearing clothes to keep the body warm, which in turn made increasingly less useful an excessive volume of body hair.

The hair of the head of primitive man was cut with stone tools or sharp silica, and remains of animal teeth used as combs were found in several archaeological research.

Since the first moment the man began to abstract himself and think about the past, the hair also had a magical significance: it was believed that the people's souls dwelt in the hair. Religious rites offering hair to the gods were frequently practiced. From there, interesting legends and mythological tales began to spread everywhere.

Hair Prehistory.,
http://thehistoryofthehairsworld.com/hair_prehistory.html.

In this chapter, I wanted to talk about the evolution of early man being all most completely covered with hair and the decline of hair on their bodies except for their heads. Later there were so many myths about hair having some supernatural significance, and I will discuss those myths in the next chapter.

CHAPTER THREE

The Role Hair Played in Africa

The Role Hair Played in Africa

In this chapter, I will dispel the horrible rumor that Africans didn't groom themselves. They took pride in their hair and their appearance. The styling of their hair was not just a style; it meant many different things and was very important to their culture. Hair is an element of Kimoyo. Kimoyo is a new term a few of us is pushing to replace the terms African Traditional Religion and African Spirituality. Those elements are **oral traditions, rites of passage, rituals, sacrifices, music, libations, masks,** and **hair**. Hair is just as important as the other elements that make up Kimoyo. If you want to know more about Kimoyo and why we are not using African Traditional Religion or African Spirituality, get my book Beautiful Lesson About Kimoyo.

After the Europeans communicated and long traded with Africans, they saw the significance in the many hairstyles and how they took pride in grooming their hair, and how hair had a spiritual connection with them. After knowing and observing them, they destroyed their love of their hair and their image during the kidnapping and enslaving of them.

Hair in Africa had a special spiritual significance. Many African cultures saw the head as the center of control, communication, and identity in the body. Hair was regarded as a source of power that personified the individual and could be used for spiritual purposes or even to cast a spell. Since it rests on the highest point on the body, the hair itself was a means to communicate with divine spirits, and it was treated in ways that were thought to bring good luck or ward off evil.

According to authors Ayana Byrd and Lori Tharps, "communication from the gods and spirits was thought to pass through the hair to get to the soul" (Bryd and Tharps 2002, 4-5). In Cameroon, for example, medicine men attached hair to containers that held their healing potions to protect them and enhance their effectiveness.

Byrd, Ayana D., and Lori L. Tharps. Hair Story: Untangling the Roots of Black Hair in America. St. Martin's Griffin, 2002.

What kind of role hair play in Africa?

"As early as the 15th century, hair was the main disseminator among different tribes and within communities of royal status, single status, married status, child status, adult status, warrior status, priest status, ethnic status, mourning, and spirituality status.

"For thousands of years, people living in Africa have devoted time and attention to styling their hair, and some traditional styles are still worn today. Ancient hieroglyphs, sculptures, and masks reveal intricate and varied hairstyles worn by people in different regions of this large continent; hair coverings do not appear on ancient sculpture drawings, which may mean that hair was supposed to be visible to other people."

Sherrow, Victoria. Encyclopedia Of Hair A Culture History. 2006.

Hairpins, beads, cowrie shells, colored cloth, flowers, and other objects have been used to adorn hair or symbolize particular stages of life or events. The Kwere of Tanzania made ornate hairpins. In Nigeria, the Ibo crafted wooded hair combs for grooming and styling their hair.

When the Europeans came into the interiors of Africa, they were impressed by the number and variety of African hairstyles. The Dutch explorer Pieter de Marees book, Description and Historical Account of the Gold Kingdom of Guinea, written on page 102, provided a detailed description and drawings of sixteen distinct hairstyles he observed in that region.

The picture below shows the royal child with a plait from the New Kingdom of ancient Egypt. The nsw bity (king of upper and lower Egypt) children wore a distinctive plait on the right side of the head). The term sidelock of youth was coined by Egyptologists, and the sidelock identified characteristics of the child in Ancient Egypt. It symbolically indicates that the wearer is a legitimate heir of Asar (Osiris). The sidelock was used as a divine attribute from at least as early as the Old Kingdom.

Rolf Gundlach, Matthias Rochholz. Ägyptische Tempel, pp. 304–307 and 310–311.

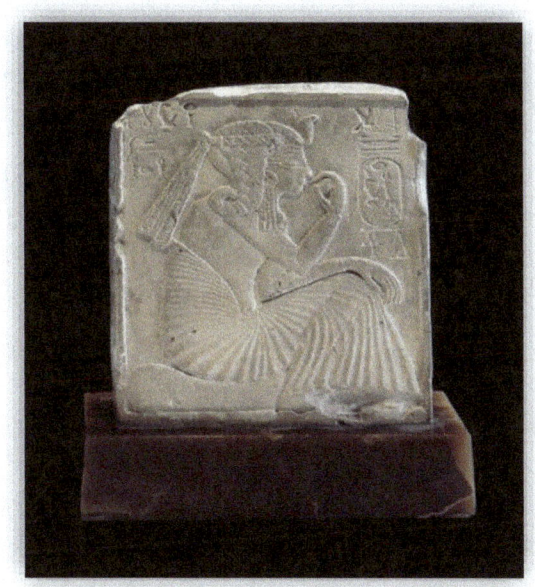

My transliteration and translation of the above artifact of Rameses II as a child with the Heru loc.

Right TRL:

nwst bity nb tAwy <wsr-mAat-stp-n-ra>

Translation: The dual King, lord of two lands <The Justice of ra is powerful, chosen of ra>

Left TRL:

mi ra Dt nHH

Translation: like ra forever and eternity

U can also see in Namibia, which is in South Africa, the Himba boys wearing this same plait on the side of their hair or a single plait to the back of the head, meaning the young men are not married yet and once they are married the men wear a cap or head wrap and unbraided hair under it.

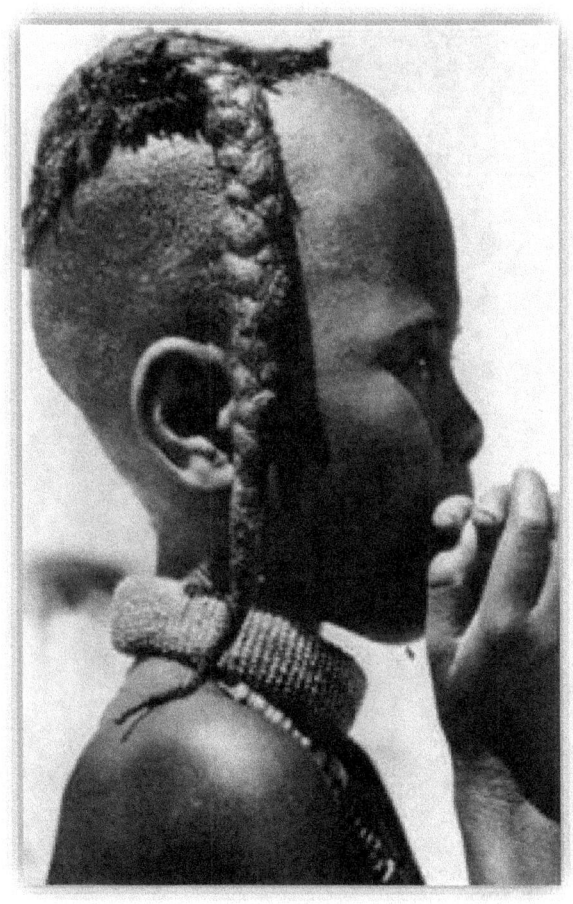

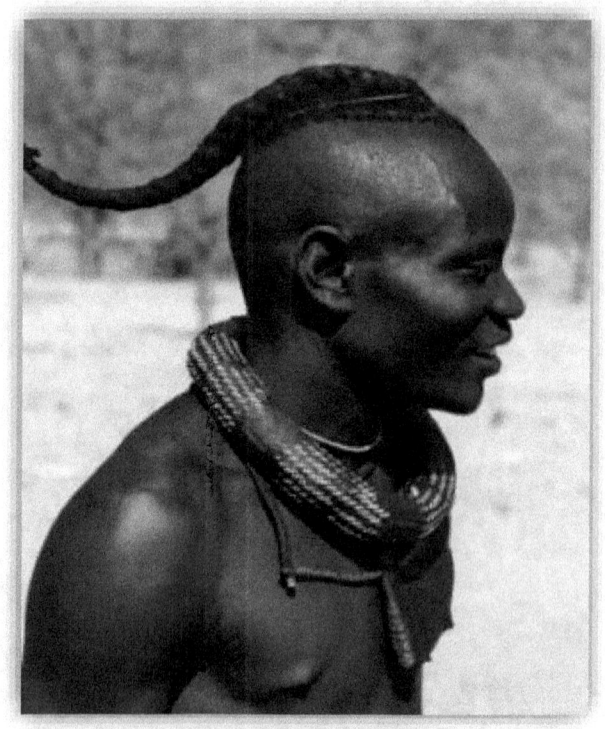

Also, according to the Himba traditions, widowed men will remove their cap or head wrap and expose un-braided hair. At the bottom is an image of a Himba man with a cap on his head, and on the next page is an image of a widowed man with unkempt hair.

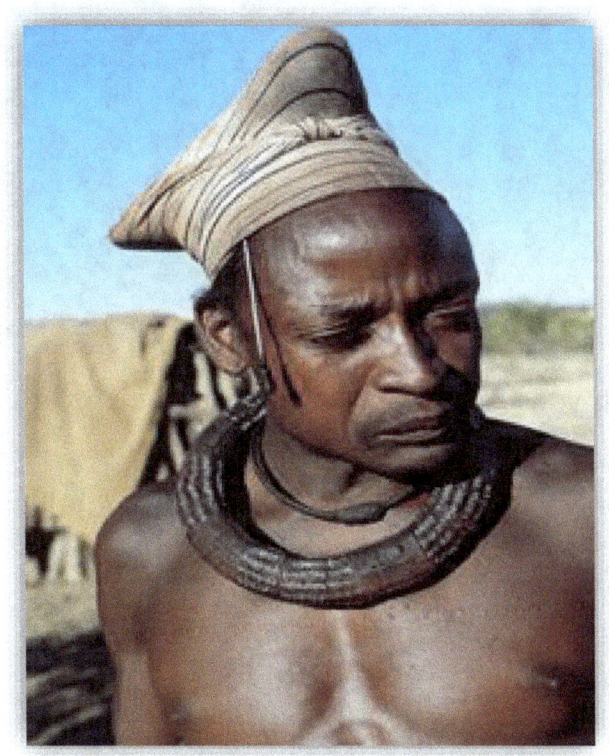

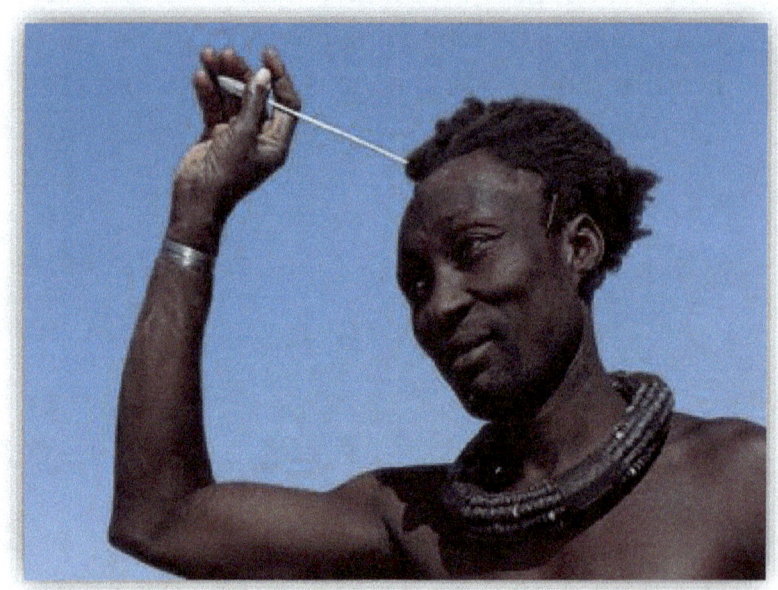

When you see an African man or woman with unkempt hair, it could mean many things, and I will discuss them later in this chapter, but, in this case, this Himba man is in mourning. In different African culture death of a loved one could result in the shaving of the head or unkempt hair.

Tradition and Ritual

"Hair has been a part of customs and rituals designed to thwart evil spirits, bring good luck, or comfort those in mourning. Many customs relate to the head and hair of newborns or the dead. For example, during the naming ceremony that takes place seven or nine days after birth, the Yoruba may shave a baby's Head to mark its passage from the spirit world into the world of the living."

"The shaved hair may be used in good luck charms or healing tonics. A dead person's head is shaved to mark the passage from this world to the next. Among Akan of Ghana, however, women and men who are most closely related to a dead person shave their heads and bodies as a sign of respect. Certain groups use hair from the deceased, or their relative, in the funeral rites. Another custom practiced in the Malagasy Republic (Formerly Madagascar), dictated that widows shave their heads. Some women had their hair removed in such a way that it could be used as a wig after the mourning period ended. Women in some parts of West Africa were expected to stop grooming their hair when they were widows to repel attention from other men since people of both genders avoided someone with untidy hair."

Sherrow, Victoria. Encyclopedia Of Hair A Culture History. 2006.

Mourning was not only for untidy hair in traditional African cultures, but men and women untidy or unkempt hair was also a sign of anti-social behavior or illness, but some African societies regard long, thick, neatly styled hair on a young woman as a sign of health, respectability, and fertility –qualities that make them desirable mates.

What we call hairdressers today hair-grooming time was a social activity, and still to this day, as women gathered to do each other's hair, it allowed them to socialize. In most communities, including those in Ghana and Senegal, hairdressers work only with members of their gender, women dress the hair of women, and men dress the hair of men. Hairdressing in Africa, which might be done daily, involves cleansing, combing, oiling, and styling into various braids, wraps, curls, twists, or other shapes, sometimes with decorative accessories. Those hair myths about black people's natural hair cannot grow long without a relaxer, or natural hair is dirty, or continental African's hair is messy and dirty is a mistruth.

So, you see, hair was a social activity, and it still is. You can walk into any hair salon and see women gathered there, socializing and getting their hair done. You will see the same thing going on in the men's barbershop.

In most African communities, women usually do the hair of women, and men do the hair of men.

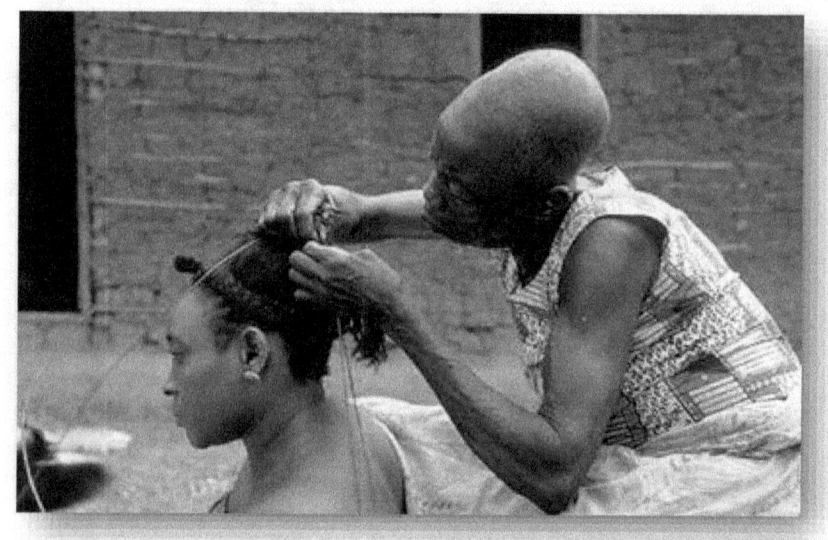

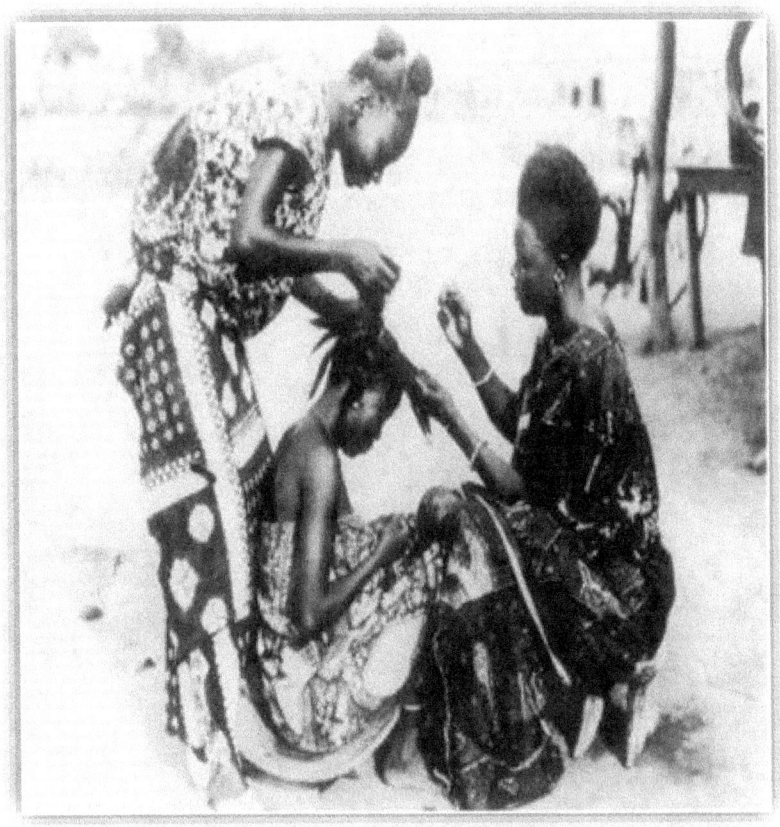

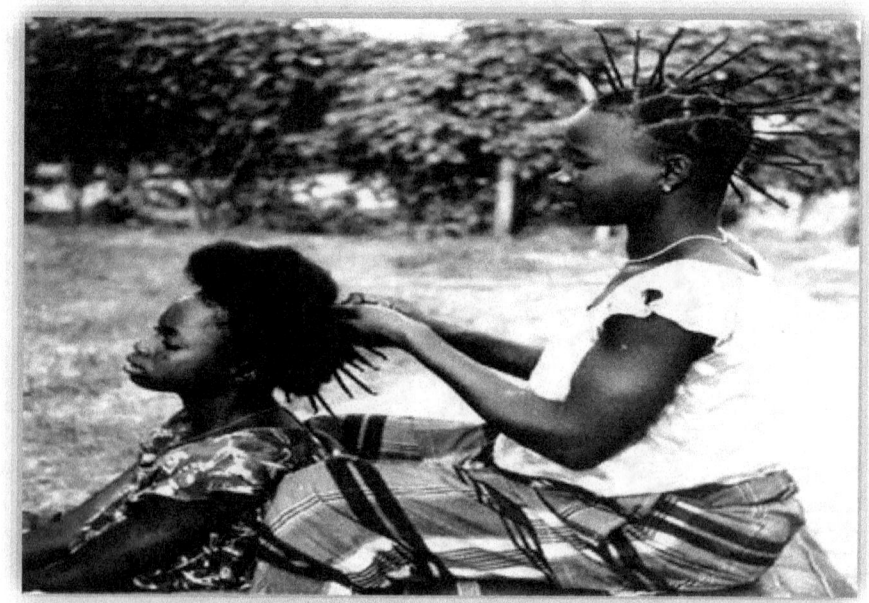

Dreadlocks from the Himba Tribe of Northwestern

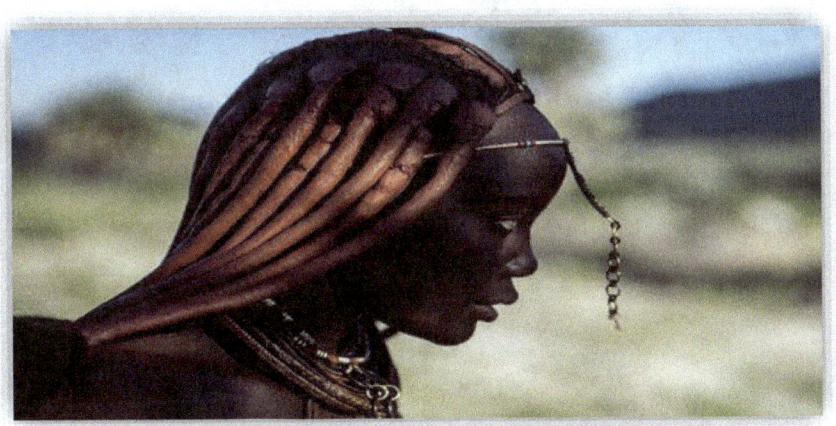

Namibia

"The Himba Tribe, whose communities are located in the northwestern region of Namibia, hair indicates one's age, life stage, and marital status. Hair is often dreadlocked with a mixture of ground ochre, goat hair, and butter. In modern times, Indian hair extensions purchased from nearby towns have been included in creating dreadlocks."

Lebo Matshego, A History Of African Women's Hairstyles
https://african.com/history-african-womens-hairstyles/

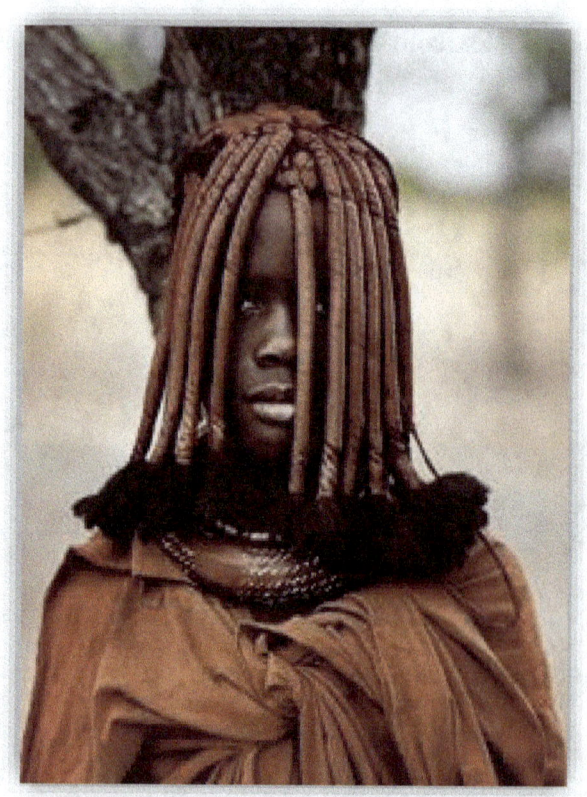

"A teenage girl who has entered puberty would usually wear braid strands or dreadlocked hair that hangs over her face, and a married woman and a new mom would wear an Erembe headdress made from animal skin over her head. A young woman ready to marry would tie back her dreadlocks, revealing her face. Interestingly, single men wear a single plaid to indicate their unmarried status, and once they marry, they cover their heads, never to unveil them in public again, except for funeral attendances."

Lebo Matshego, A History Of African Women's Hairstyles https://african.com/history-african-womens-hairstyles/

Ready Get Married

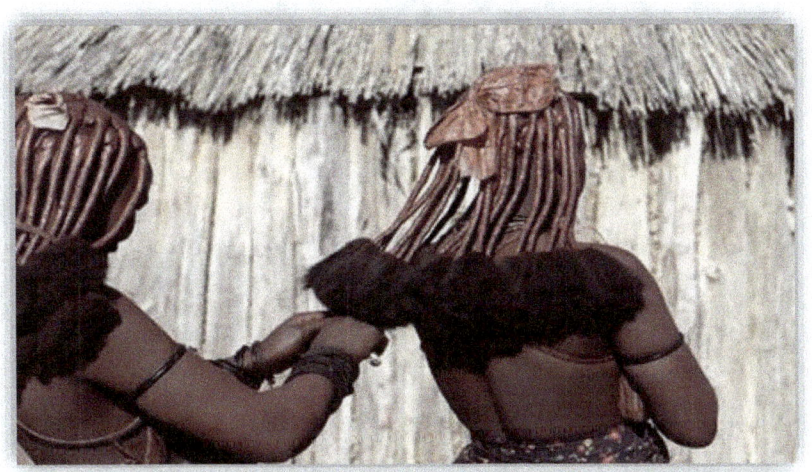

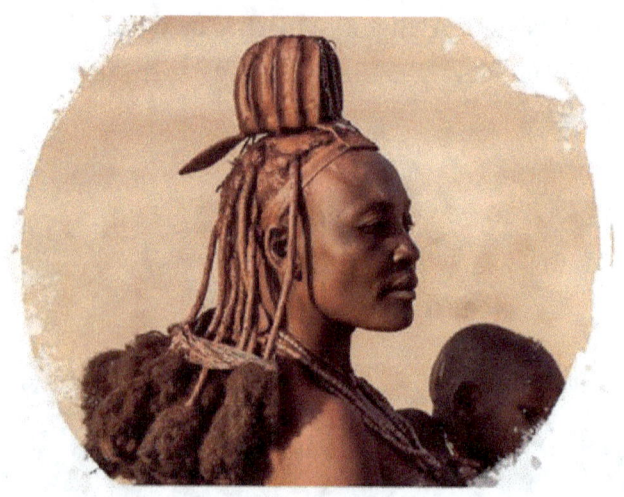

Once a Himba woman is married and a new mom, she wears a headdress called an Erembe. This Erembe lets everyone in the community know she is married. In most African societies, when you mention children, you mention marriage in the same breath. Marriage is the most important rite of passage.

Ochre dreadlocks of the Hamar Tribe in Ethiopia

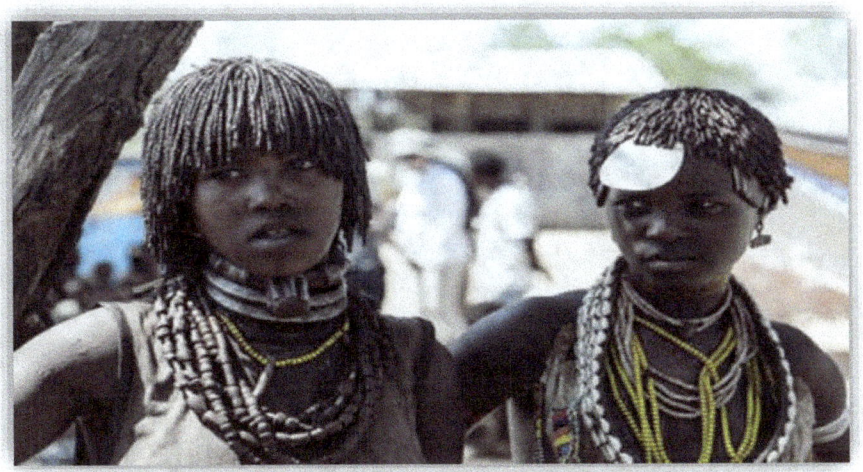

"The Hamar Tribe is a pastoral community with an estimated population of 20,000 that live in Ethiopia's Omo Valley. Women are often adorned with colorful beaded jewelry, and they mostly wear their hair in thin ochre dreadlocks created with water and binding resin. The twisted tresses are known as goscha. Pre-adolescent girls wear their hair in cornrows that are decorated with beads."

Lebo Matshego, A History Of African Women's Hairstyles
https://african.com/history-african-womens -hairstyles/

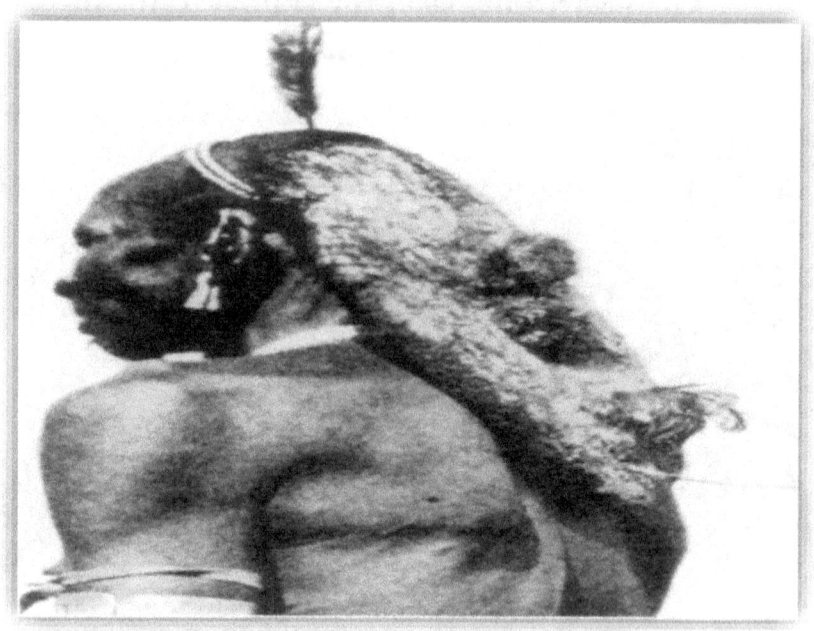

Among the Asante: "Priests' hair was allowed to grow into long matted dreadlocks in a style known as mpesempese (a term sometimes translated as 'I don't like it'). Uncut hair is usually associated with dangerous behavior: madmen let their locks grow, and the same hairstyle was worn by royal executioners.

When most people think of dreadlocks, they think the hairstyle originated in Jamaica with the Rastafarians. Dreadlocks are not unique to Jamaica and Rastafarians. The dreadlocks hairstyle originated in Africa and was worn by various tribes there. On page 56, we saw the Himba women with their thick dreadlocks; on page 57, we saw the Hamar women with their thin dreadlocks; and on page 58, we saw an Asante priest with matted dreadlocks. The Himba tribe is from Southern Africa, the Hamar tribe is from East Africa, and the Asante tribe is from West Africa, and in North Africa, there are Egyptian reliefs with Egyptian wearing dreadlocks, so you see, dreadlocks were not just worn in one region of Africa,

Egyptian relief depiction of Amenmose and his wife Depet (relief is now in Louvre museum)

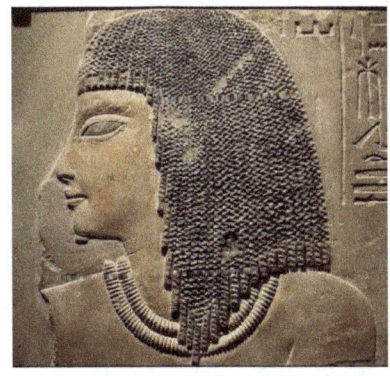 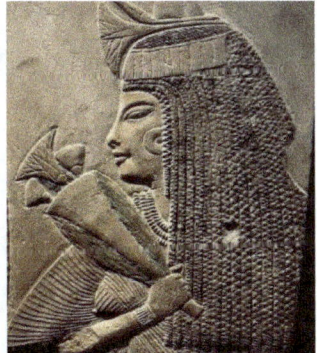

The earliest tribe with this dreadlock hairstyle can be attributed to the Maasai tribesmen of Kenya. Many of the warriors of this tribe wore this hairstyle. These men sometimes dyed their hair red with root extracts.

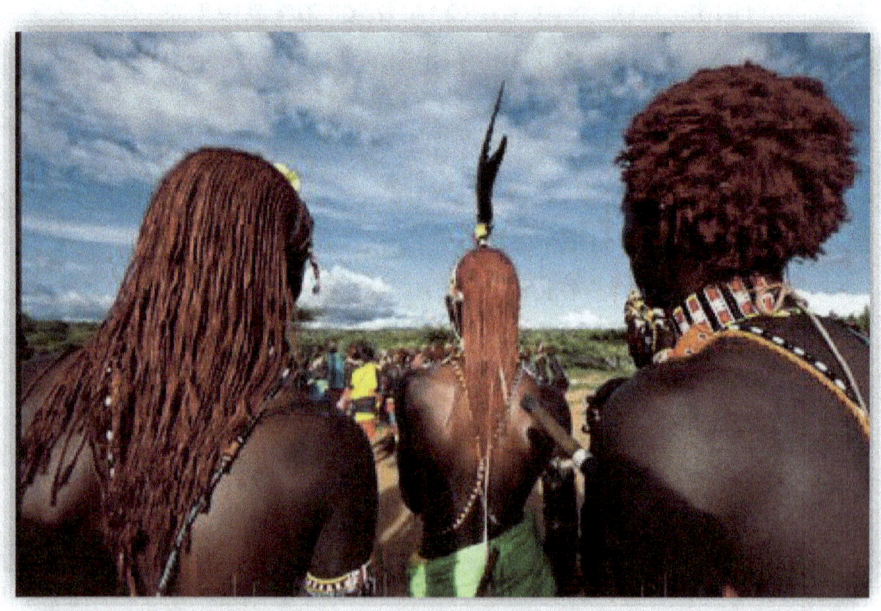

There was something thrown out on my sister Ladosha Wright's Monday shows on Youtube about dreadlocks, and I just want to clarify one thing. I can't quite remember exactly what Ladosha brilliant cost-host said, but it was something along the lines of dreadlocks being created or worn for resistance or rebellion against European powers. When I first heard her say that, I disagreed, but there is some truth to what she said, but the origin of dreadlocks is in Africa, and it is a tradition for some tribes in Africa to wear this hairstyle referred to as dreadlocks. So, the reason I disagreed was the style was worn way before they unexpectedly experienced the Europeans.

The dreadlocks hairstyle first appeared in Jamaica during post-emancipation. It was a means of defiance for ex-slaves to rebel against Eurocentrism that was forced on them.

The hairstyle was originally referred to as a "dreadful" hairstyle by the Euro-centric Jamaican society. It later evolved to the term now used: Dreadlocks. Jamaicans also use the term Natty Dreadlock. Ladosha, brilliant co-host, was right that the hairstyle called dreadlocks was used for defiance or open resistance. I just want to make clear that the dreadlock hairstyle did not originate on the island of Jamaica. Let me make this clear those melanated people in Jamaica or Africans, and they arrive there via slave ships.

Famous Jamaican Dreadlock Rastafarian

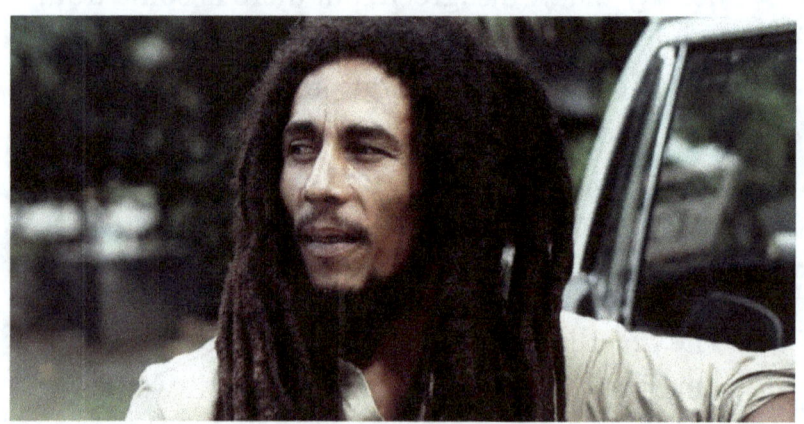

Bob Marley

Braids and beads from the Fulani Tribe of the Sahel Region and West Africa

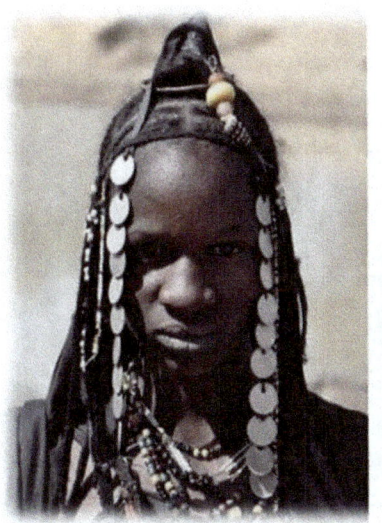 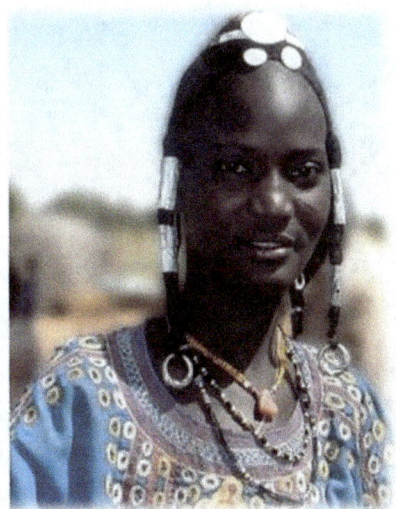

The Fula, or Fulani Tribe, is the largest nomadic pastoral community in the world that populate West Africa and the Sahel Region.

A very traditional hairstyle for women includes long hair being put into five long braids that either hang or are looped on the sides, with a coiffure in the middle of the head. Hair is decorated with beads and cowrie shells. A tradition that is passed through the generations to women and young girls includes attaching the family's silver coins and amber onto braids as a heritage symbol as well as for aesthetic purposes.

65

Braids and beads from the Wodaabe Tribe of the Sahel Region and West Africa

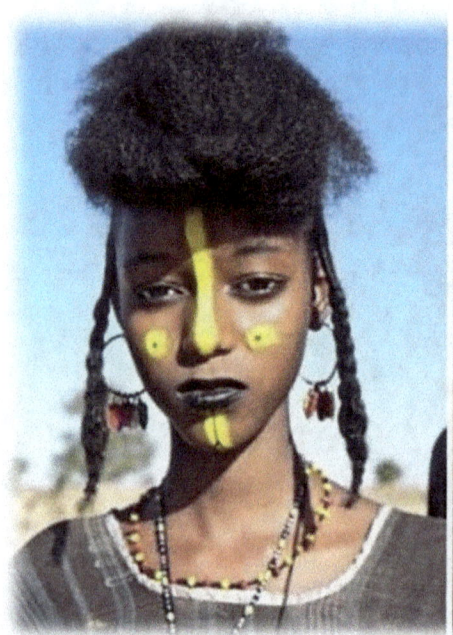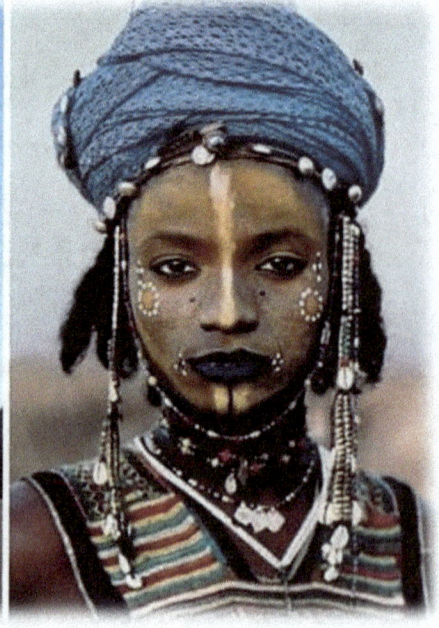

Tribe, also residing in the Sahel Region and West Africa. They are a pastoral nomadic tribe with an estimated population of 100,000. The young girls and women of the tribe wear a braided hairstyle similar to Fulani women, consisting of two braids on either side of the head or a few braids on their hair and a coiffure in the middle. The hair is usually decorated with beads and cowrie shells.

As a young teenager and young adult, I wore braids and beads in my hair for years. I had no clue that our people in Africa wore braids in beads. I only knew what the commercial showed me in between my favorite shows after school. Those images were negative images of pop-belly Africans with unkempt hair. I teach my son to don't believe everything on tv, especially when it comes to our people. Braids and beads are still popular among the young folks.

Locs have become super popular over the years, and they decorated their locs with cowrie shells. Cowrie shells are also worn in the hair of our brothers and sisters in Africa. I have locs, my wife has locs, my stepdaughter has locs, and my son now has locs. My wife and stepdaughter wear cowrie shells in their hair, and they had no clue that our brothers and sisters wore beads and cowrie shells in their hair for centuries.

Beads and cowrie shells are important in African culture. They not only wore them in their hair but on their masks and clothes, and they even decorated their musical instruments with them. Cowrie shells and Beads were also used as currency at want point in history.

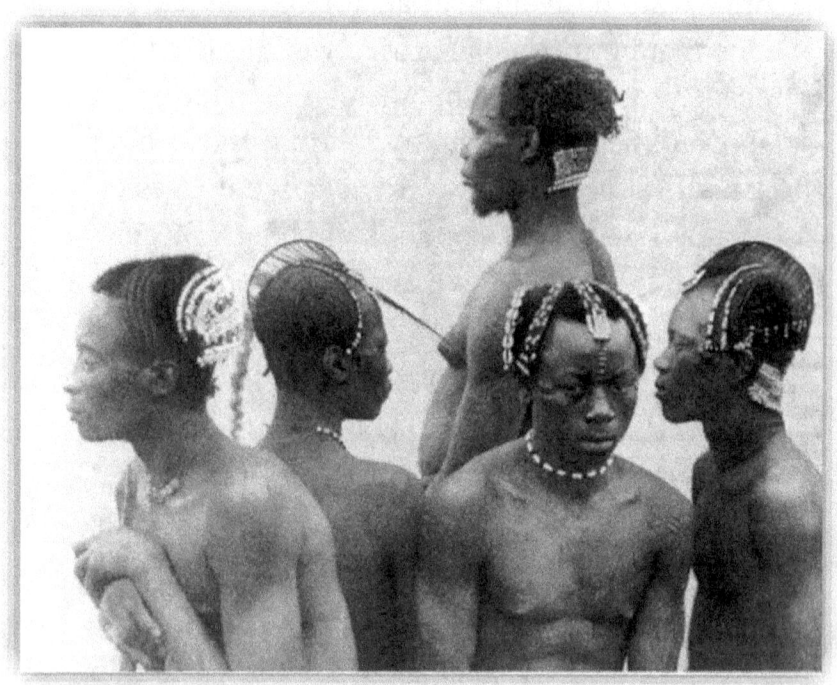

Sango men wearing cowrie shells in their hair.
Sango, Upper Mobangi River, Democratic
Republic of Congo.

African Styles

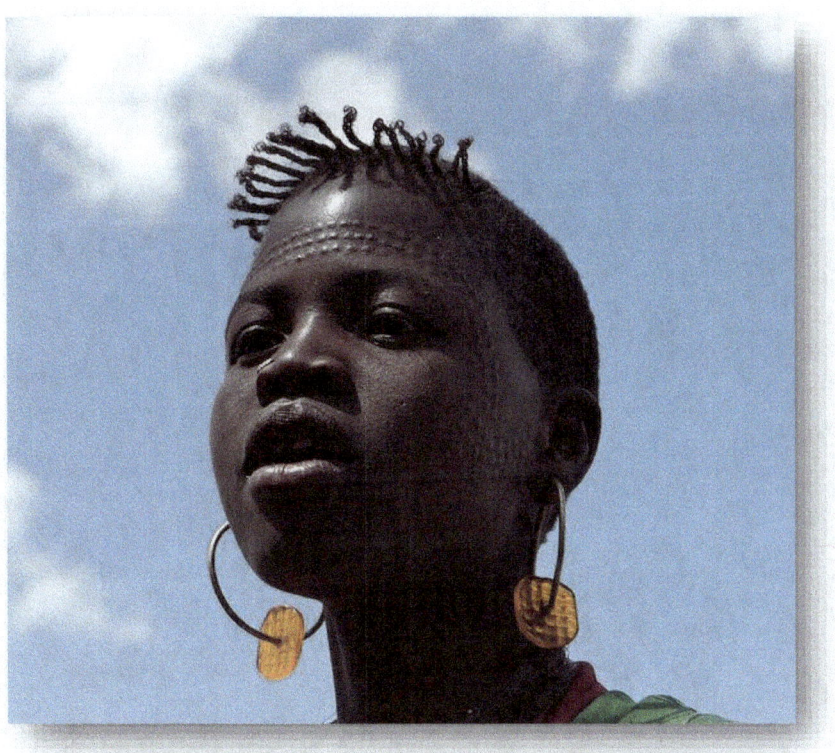

Karamojong Hairstyle

African Styles

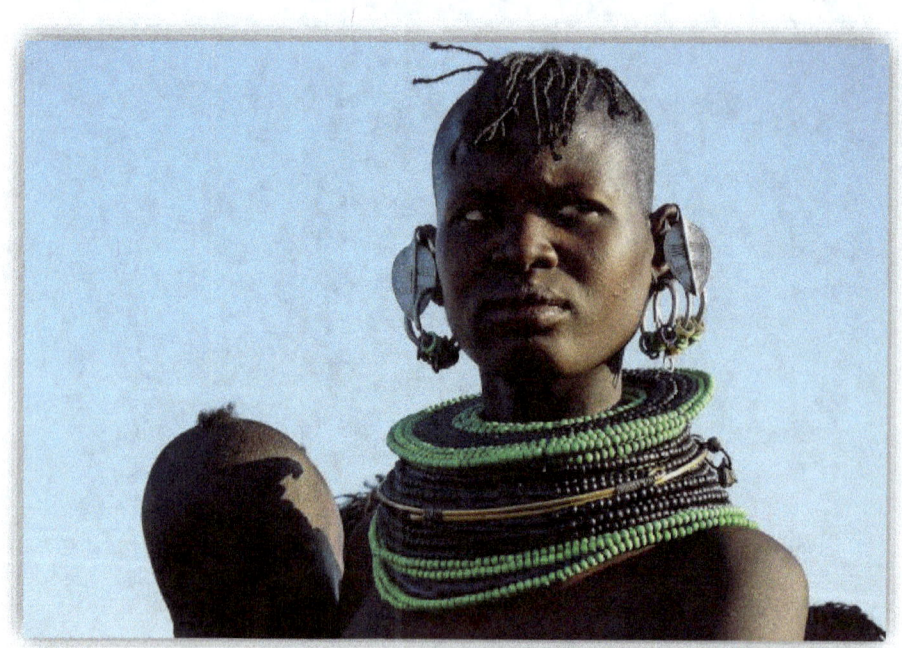

Turkana Hairstyle

African Styles

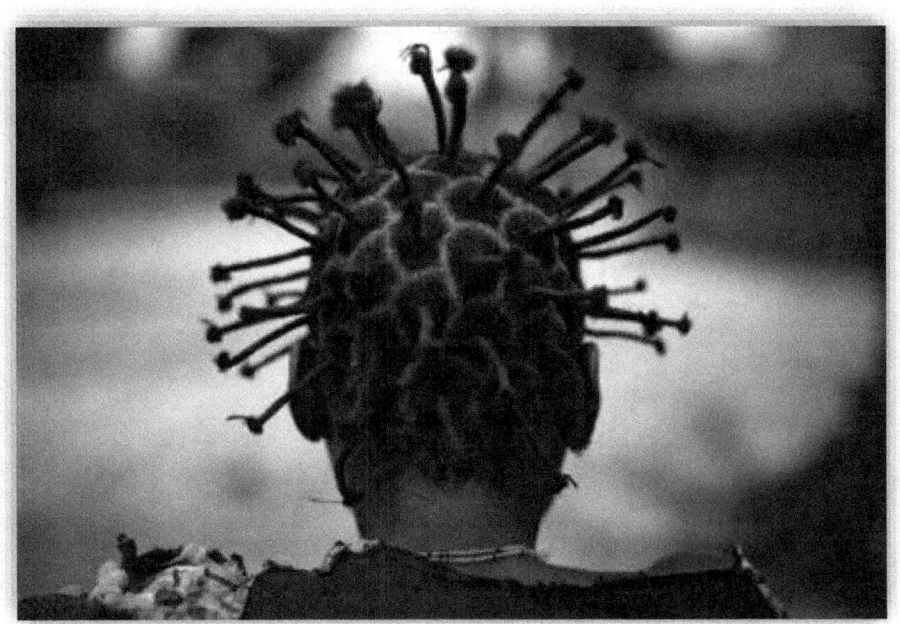

Congo hair

African Styles

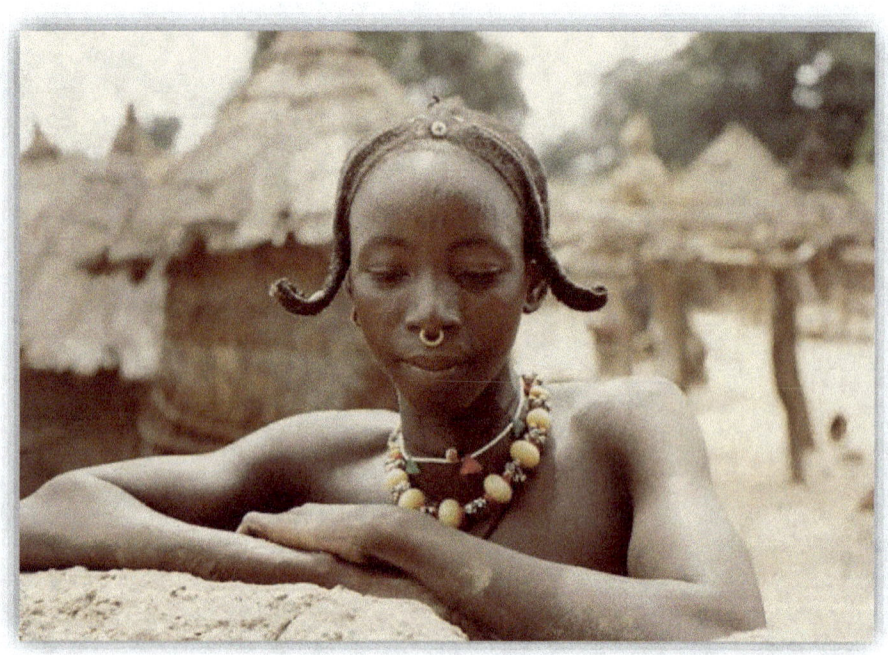

Bamana woman hairstyle

African Styles

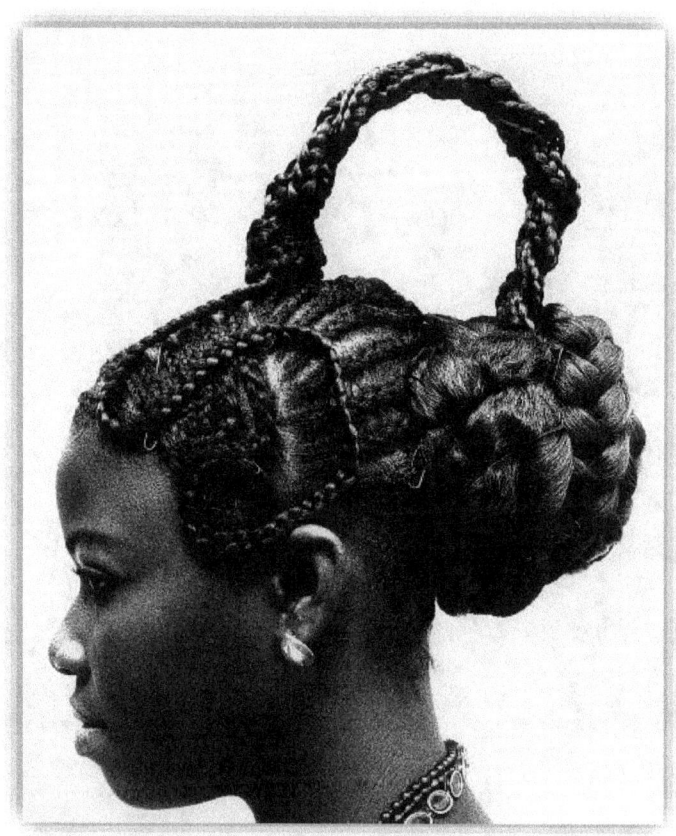

Nigerian hairstyle

African Styles

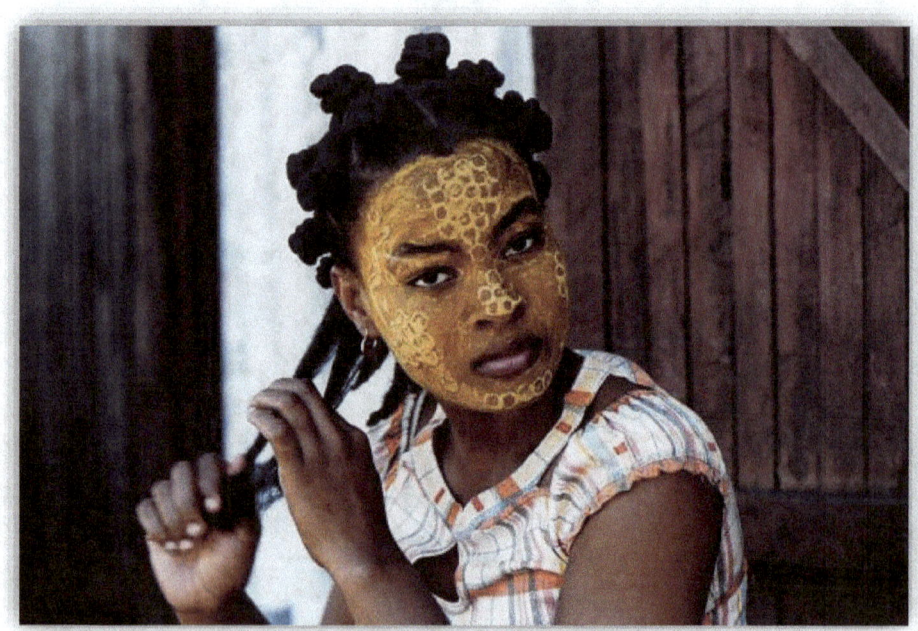

Skavalava Hairstyle

African Styles

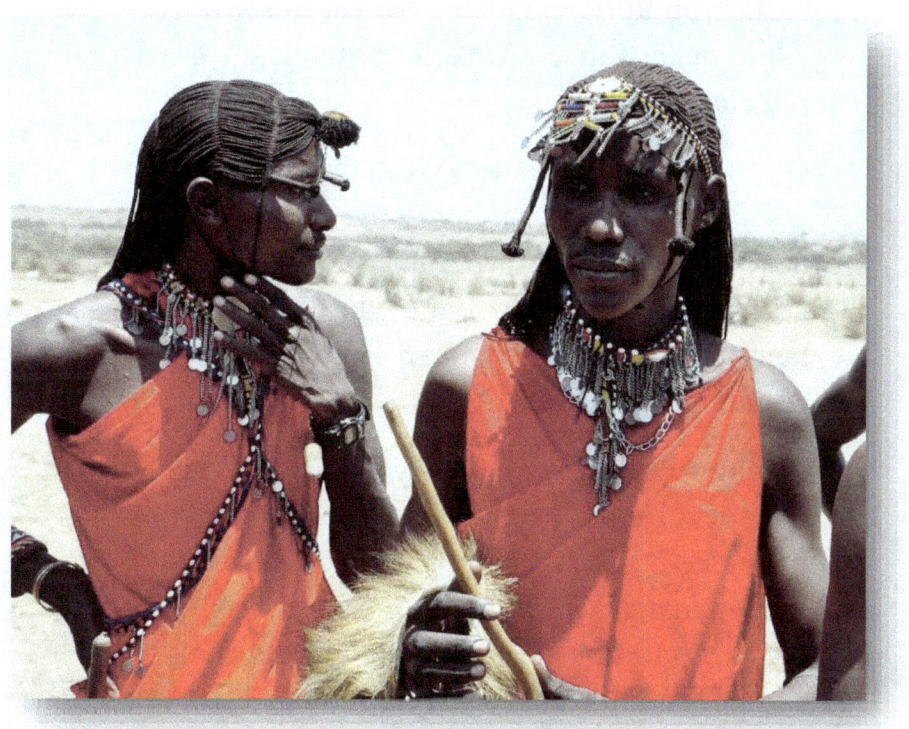

Maasai men hairstyles

African hairstyles have revealed a person's age, birthplace, clan membership, marital status, and occupation, among other things. For instance, Kuramo men of Nigeria could be recognized by their partially shaved heads, with just one tuft of hair on top. Among the Masai, women and children traditionally keep their heads shaved, while male warriors wear long braids dyed with red clay.

Only community leaders wore the most elaborate hairstyle, and only the ruler wore a headdress. Crowns were made from leather, gold, beads, and fancy braids. Priests also wear hairstyles that set them apart from other community members.

Young women may wear styles that show they are open to marriage, whereas married women's hairstyles show they are unavailable. Before marriage., Ibo girls in present-day Nigeria traditionally used clay, ground coal, and palm oil to shape their hair into a horn shape that bends toward their brows.

Girls in Senegal may wear braids and whimsical styles, while married women have plainer, covered styles.

In Kenya, young Turkana men spent hours getting elaborate hairstyles that show they have completed the initiation rites for adulthood.

Among some ancient societies, African men wore their hair in distinctive styles when they were about to go to war. This signals their families to prepare for possible death.

Sherrow, Victoria. Encyclopedia Of Hair A Culture History. 2006.

There are tons of pictures I could have put in this chapter. Our brothers and sisters had many hairstyles that resembled some of the hairstyles we wear right now. They kept their hair neat and groomed. I hope this chapter clears up the silly misinformation that Africans do not groom or wash their hair. Pride was taken greatly into the hair, and this was a lifestyle and their way of life.

CHAPTER FOUR

Hair In African Art

Hair In African Art

Hair is everywhere in African culture and was not just seen on top of people's heads in Africa but on their artwork as well. Again, hair was important and used in many different ways. They even made clothes out of hair. We today think hair is just hair and serve the purpose of just being on top of our head and cutting it and styling it to make us feel and look good. There is nothing wrong with feeling good, but hair just meant more in African Culture.

All of these stylistic possibilities are represented in statues and masks, for the most part, in an idealized way. In many African figures, the head is huge in relation to the rest of the body. This disproportion can be attributed to the concept that the identity of the supernatural being or ancestor is largely determined by the shape, finish, and embellishment of the head, including scarification, facial paint, and the form of the coiffure. Many figures, masks, and prestige objects display complex hairstyles that are often symbolic of the status of the ancestor portrayed, the significance of the spiritual force embodied by the masquerader, or the secular importance of a ruler.

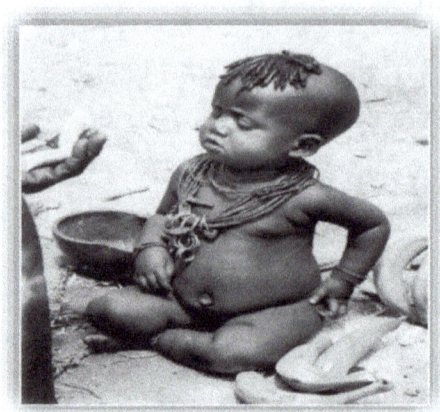 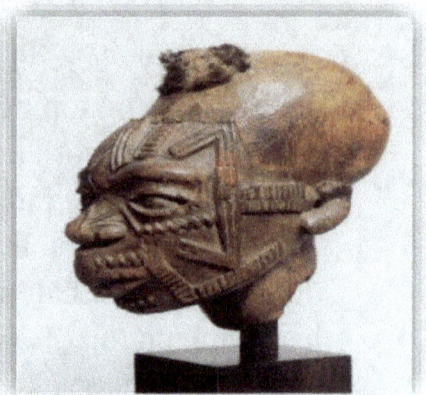

Head. Makonde, Tanzania. Wood, human hair; 16cm (6.3"). Drs. Jean and Noble Endicott. The hair atop this head fragment reflects the naturalism of Makonde art.

Infants and toddlers of both sexes may have their heads shaved except for tufts of hair left to protect the fontanel. Girls receive or make dolls depicting local hairdos; these figures promote their adult responsibilities as mothers. A. B. Ellis, writing in 1887, reports that an Akan girl "announcing her eligibility for marriage...is carefully adorned with all the ornaments and finery in possession of the family, and frequently with others borrowed for the occasion. The hair is covered with gold ornaments" (1887:235)

Sieber, Roy, and Frank Herreman. "Hair in African Art and Culture." African Arts, vol. 33, no. 3, 2000, https://doi.org/10.2307/3337689.

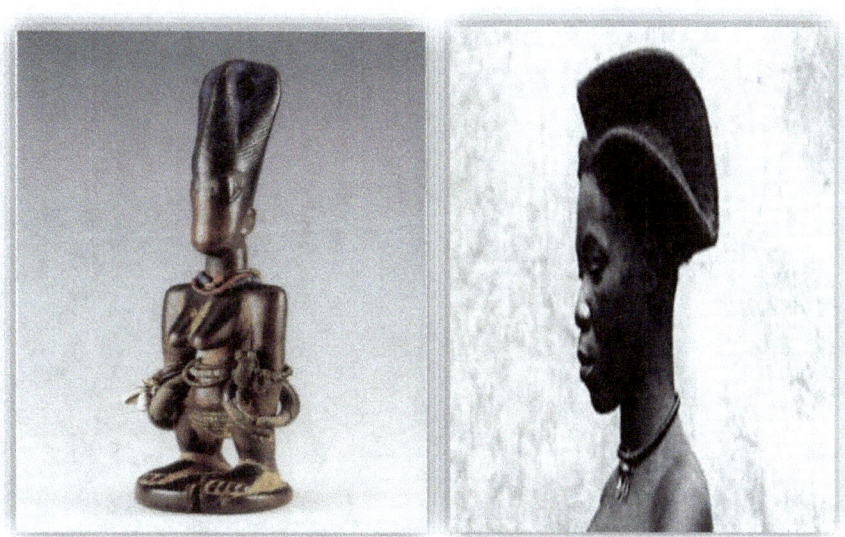

Twin figure (ibeji). Yoruba, Nigeria. Wood, metal, beads, fiber; 32.5cm (12.8"). Private collection, Belgium. This ibeji is wearing a suku ("knotted hair") coiffure, so called because the braids terminate in a short or long knot on the crown of the head.

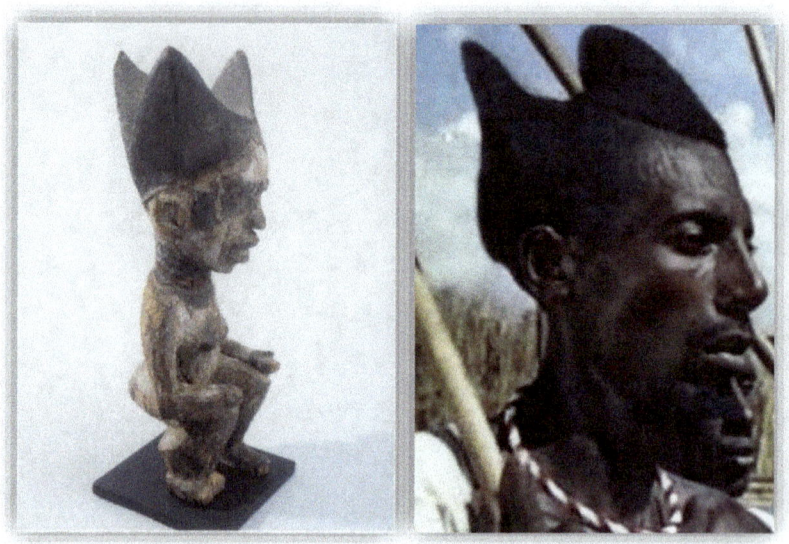

Figure. Igbo or Ejagham, Nigeria. Wood; 24cm (9.4"). Collection of Toby and Barry Hecht. The large head reflects the belief that the identity of an ancestor or supernatural being can be determined by the shape, finish, and embellishments of the head, including the coiffure.

It is not difficult to point out extremes in hairstyles, ranging from minimal to elaborately detailed, in the incredibly diverse formal language of African sculpture. The coiffure of the Kuba doll is suggested by a simple hairline, recurrent in ornamental cups, cosmetics boxes, and royal statues. In contrast, the hair depicted on a crest mask from the Cross River region is indisputably the center of attention, with several corkscrew braids radiating from the head in different directions. The coiffure helps to create a distinctly dramatic appearance for the moving masked figure.

Both these cases indicate that the African sculptor represents hairstyles conceptually rather than mimetically. This approach is entirely in accord with one of the principal characteristics of African sculpture, which is that it never copies exactly from nature.

The artists are often inspired by what they know rather than what they see. They do not hesitate to accentuate what is considered important in their cultures.

Sieber, Roy, and Frank Herreman. "Hair in African Art and Culture." African Arts, vol. 33, no. 3, 2000, https://doi.org/10.2307/3337689.

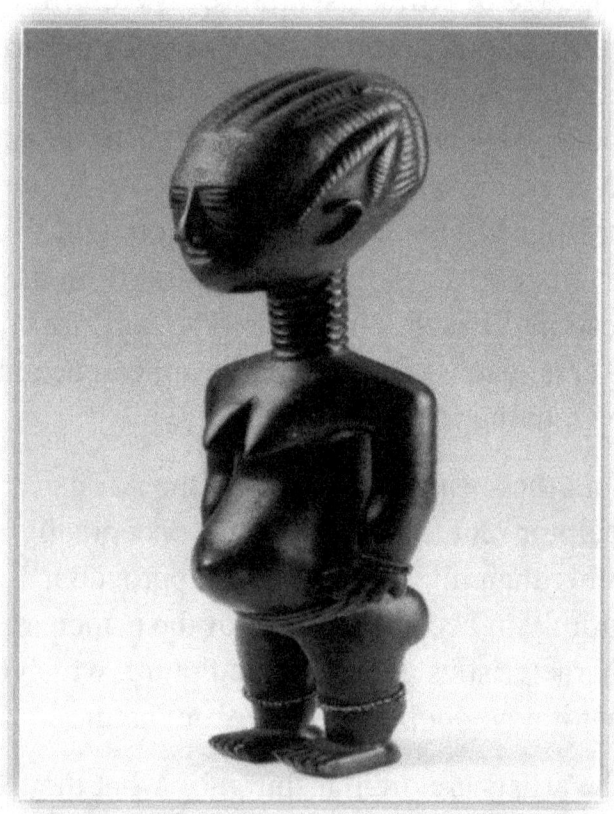

Figure. Asante, Ghana. Wood, beads; 37.5cm(14.8").Henau
Collection, Antwerp.

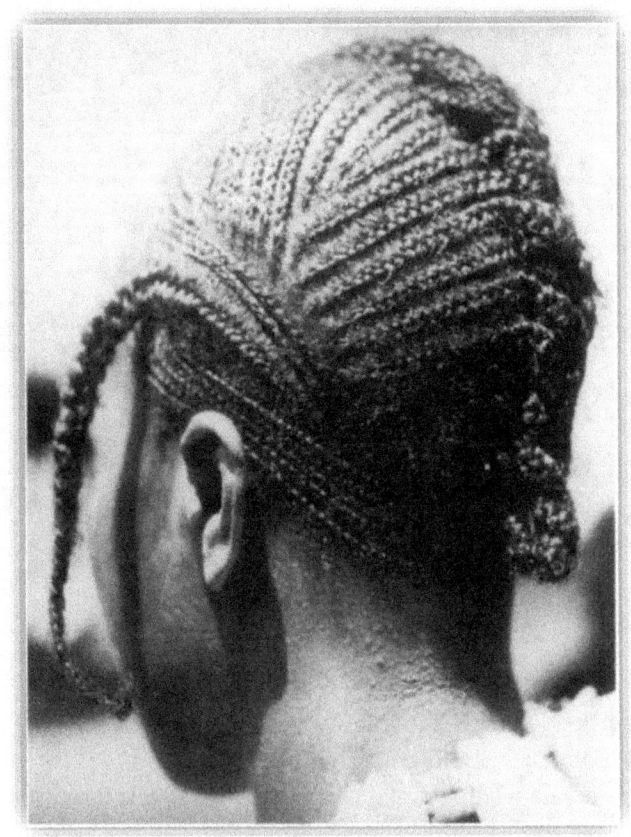

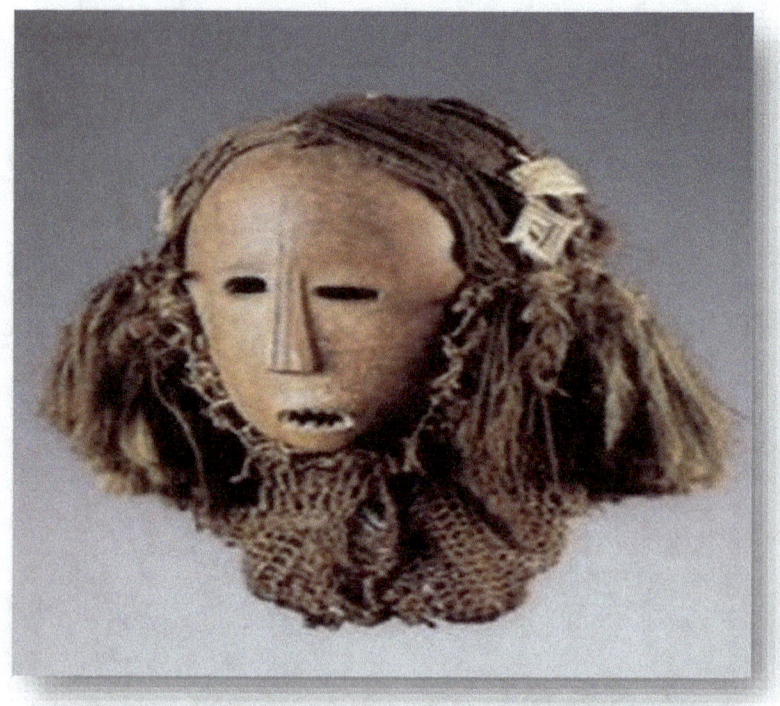

Face mask. Ngangela, Angola. Wood, fiber; 27cm (10.6").
Private collection, Belgium. Fiber braids attached to this
mask re-create a hairstyle favored by the Ngangela

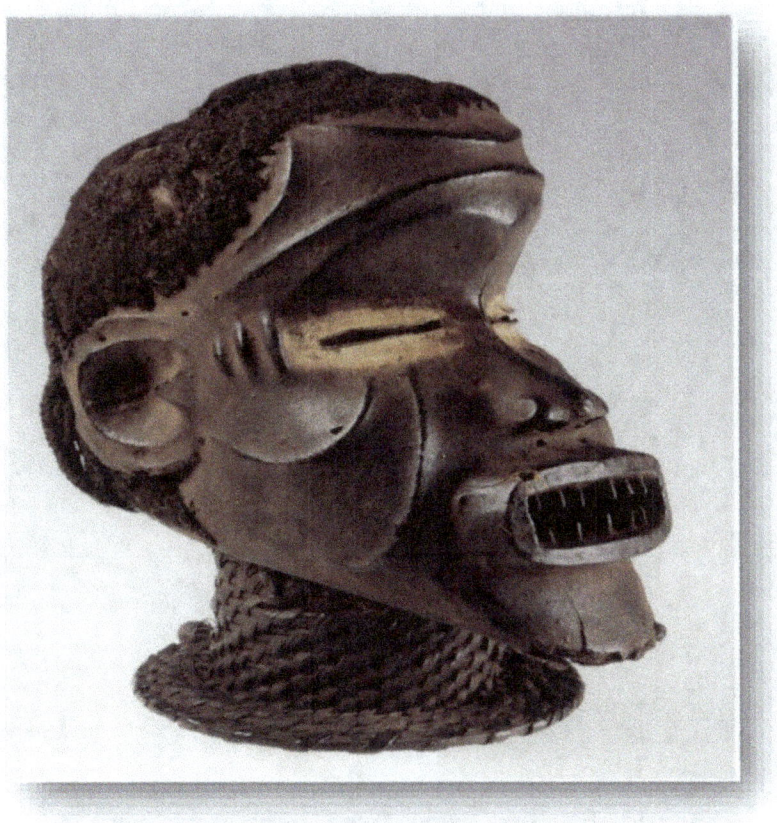

Crest mask. Ejagham, Nigeria. Wood, skin, human hair, basketry; 26cm (10.2'). Henau Collection, Antwerp

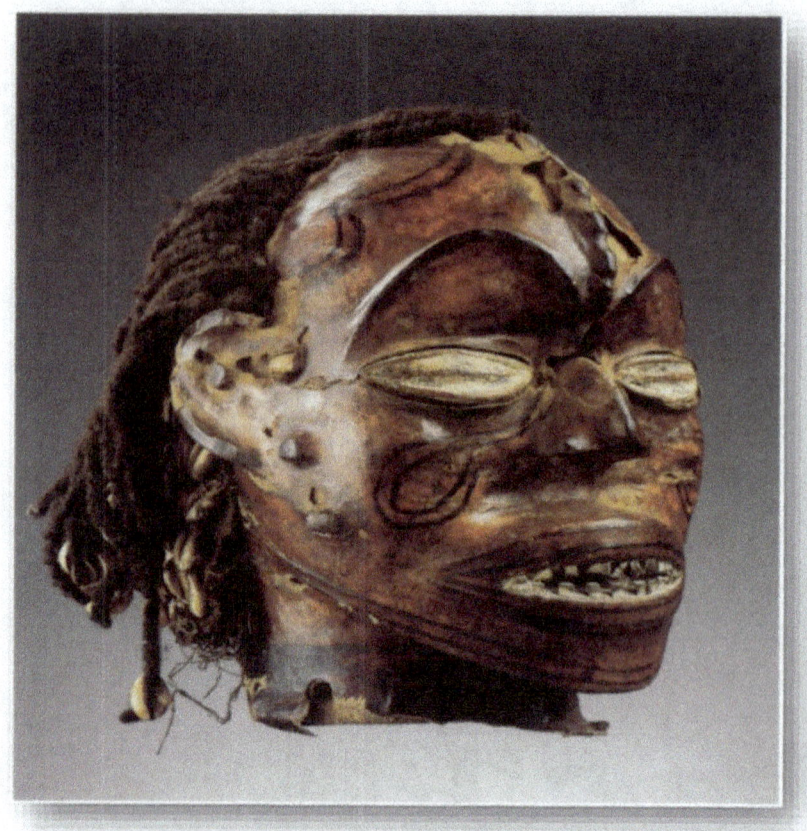

Crest mask. Ejagham, Nigeria. Wood, skin, human hair, cowrie shells; 26cm (10.2"). Collection of Rolf and Christina Miehler.

In the Cross River region, crest masks are covered with tightly stretched goat or antelope skin. Hair may be represented in various ways: through coloring, wooden pegs suggesting tufts of hair.

Neck rest

Neck rests (often called headrests or pillows) have been used all over Africa to protect one's coiffure during sleep. They were found as part of grave furniture in ancient Egypt and Nubia. The concept may have spread from the north throughout the continent, but it is by no means impossible that the move was from south to north in prehistoric times. The variety of forms does suggest long, separate evolutions.

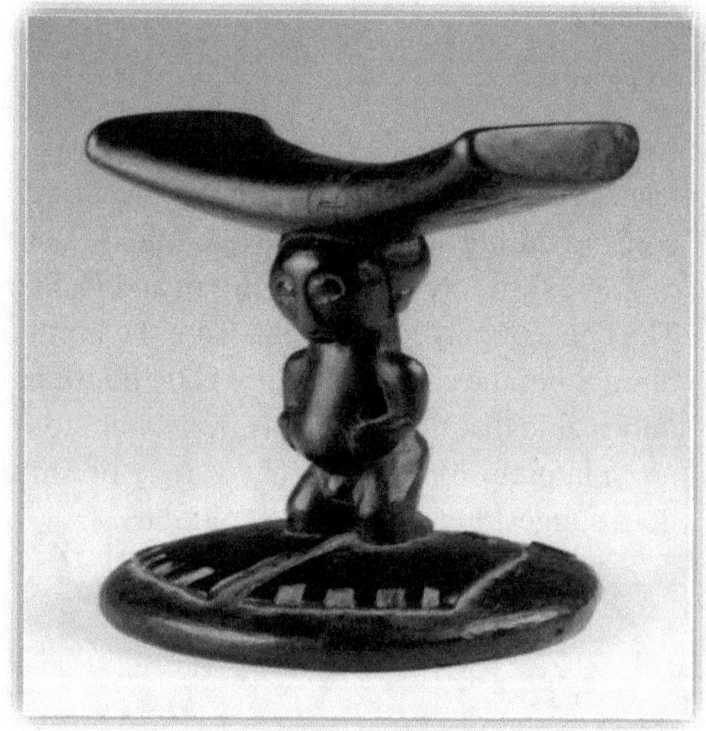

Neckrest. Luba, Democratic Republic of the Congo. Wood; 17cm (6.7"). Private collection

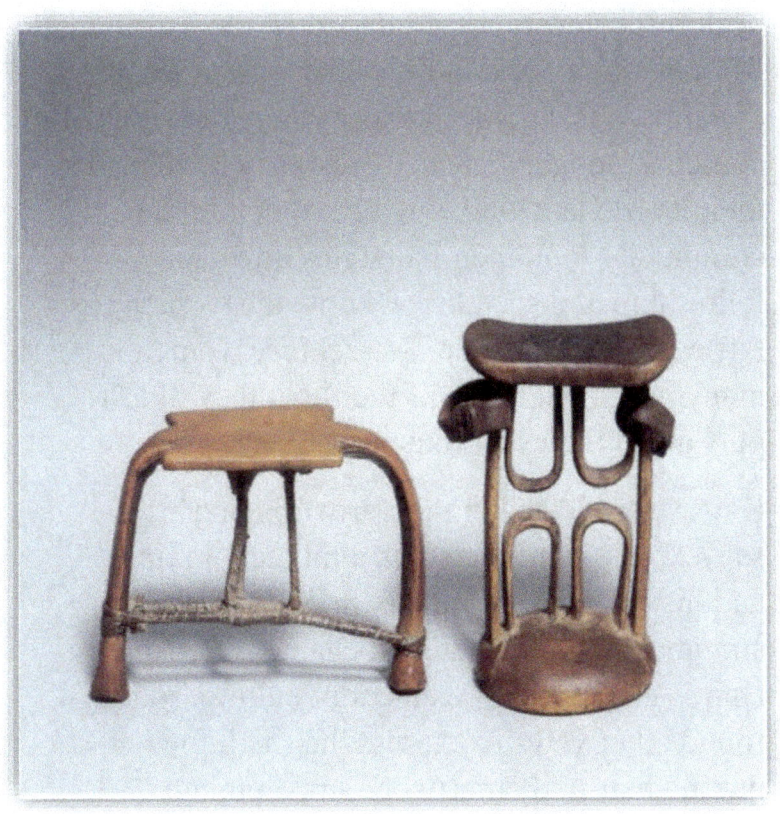

Neckrests. Left: Bari, Sudan. Wood, leather, 12.7cm (5"). Right: East Africa. Wood, leather; 16.5cm (6.5"). Collection of Roy and Sophia Sieber.

As we can see, these neck rests came in handing when lying down, resulting in the hairstyle lasting for weeks or even months. The neck rests elevate the head to keep the hairdo from being crushed during sleep. This idea at this time was a game changer where the styles could last longer. The neck rest may have made their hairdo last long, but the women in the community took their hairstyles down to fellowship and socialize. I know the women in Africa are not like our 21st-century women in many ways, but that hair tho, I bet they didn't play about their hair like our women.

Hair was reflected in their artwork, and art is self-expression; it captures a moment in time and historical events and stimulates creativity and imagination. I stated in chapter three that Hair is an important element of culture, so they found other ways to express their hair by putting hair in their artwork and clothing.

CHAPTER FIVE

Myths on African Hair

Myths on African Hair

Hair comes in all different colors, shapes, and sizes. Let's start with 4 types of hair textures and shapes.

- Type 1 = Straight hair – has little to no shape and is difficult to hold curls or waves.
- Type 2 = Wavy hair – starts to have some shape instead of falling flat like straight hair.
- Type 3 = Curly hair – ranges from loose curls to corkscrew curls.
- Type 4 = Kinky or Coily hair – tight coils and Z-angle coils that resemble zigzags.

These 4 types break down into further subcategories going from A to C. A is the loosest, and C is the curliest. Identifying your hair type is essential when learning how to properly care for and style your hair.

Ethnicity and Hair Profiles

There are 3 ethnic-hair profiles. Different ethnic groups have hair that grows in a different way and surprisingly speeds too. They each have their own common characteristics, including color, texture, and structure. These ethnic-hair profiles determine the characteristics of Asian, Caucasian, and African hair. Due to their differences, we must understand that hair does not grow in the same way or speed as those of different ethnic origins. The three ethnic hair profiles are Asian, Caucasian, and African. Let's go over each profile's characteristics and their differences.

Asian hair

Asian hair is usually black and very straight because it grows perpendicularly to the scalp. Asian hair is the fastest-growing hair, at a rate of approximately 1.4 centimeters per month. A strand of Asian hair has a somewhat round, even shape but has the lowest density of the three ethnicities.

Caucasian hair

Caucasian hair is the most diverse of the three ethnicities in terms of characteristics. It can be straight, wavy, or curly, and its color can vary from blond to black. Caucasian hair grows diagonally to the scalp, approximately 1.2 centimeters per month. A strand of Caucasian hair is oval in shape and has the highest density of the three ethnic profiles. This means that Caucasian hair is typically the fullest of the three.

African hair

Most often, African hair is characterized by tight curls and kinks. It grows almost parallel to the scalp and has the slowest growth rate at 0.9 centimeters per month. The reason for it having the slowest growth rate of the three profiles is due to the spiral structure that causes it to curl upon itself during growth. An African hair strand has a flat shape and is in the middle of the three profiles in terms of density.

Dasia. Black Hair Types. Afro Lovely, 2022.

While there are multiple differences between the three profiles, there are also multiple similarities. All hair is composed of a cortex, a cuticle, a medulla, and the keratin protein.

Black Hair Myths

Myth 1: African hair is wiry and very coarse

Myth 2: African hair is dry

Myth 3: African hair can't be grown long

Myth 4: Natural Hair is Expensive to Maintain

Myth 5: Natural Hair Is Hard to Manage

These are 5 myths, but there are many more I could have listed but let's deal with a few of the myths.

Myth: Natural Hair is Hard to Manage

According to Del Sandeen, who is a writer who focuses on Black women's issues, including haircare, says Natural, textured hair can seem hard to manage if you attempt to treat it like straight hair. If you use the same tools and expect the same results that you would on straightened hair, you're going to be disappointed. However, once you learn to treat natural hair in a way that doesn't try to change or alter it, it can be as manageable as any other type of hair. As Sango says, "Give yourself time to connect with your hair. The more you explore by using different ingredients and practicing different styling techniques, the easier it will become to manage."

Sandeen, Del. "7 Myths about Natural Black Hair." Byrdie, Byrdie, 26 Dec. 2021, https://www.byrdie.com/myths-about-natural-black-hair-400343.

Myths: African hair can't be grown long

This myth is B.S. Our sisters in Africa have been growing their natural hair down their backs. Let's look at Chad in West Africa. The Basara Arab women are known to have very long, naturally coarse hair that famously goes passed their rear ends. They cover their hair in a homemade mixture that keeps their hair super moisturized and lubricated, which is the reason given for why they say their hair never breaks, even from childhood.

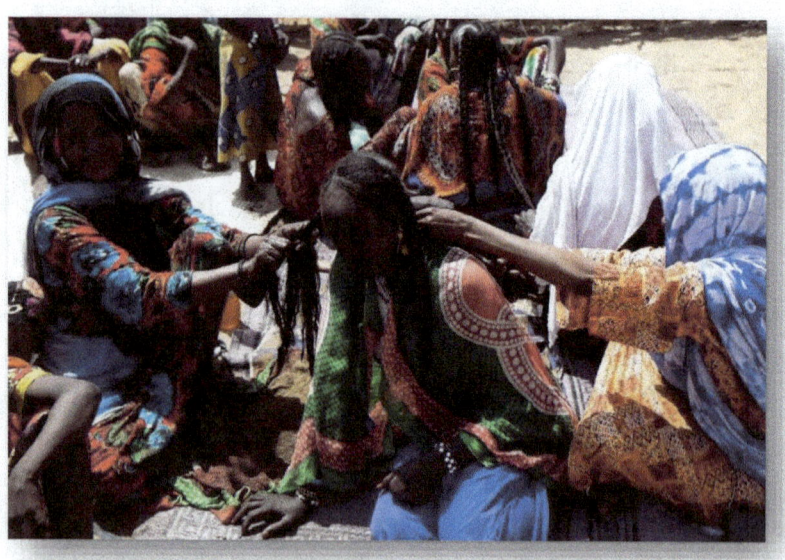

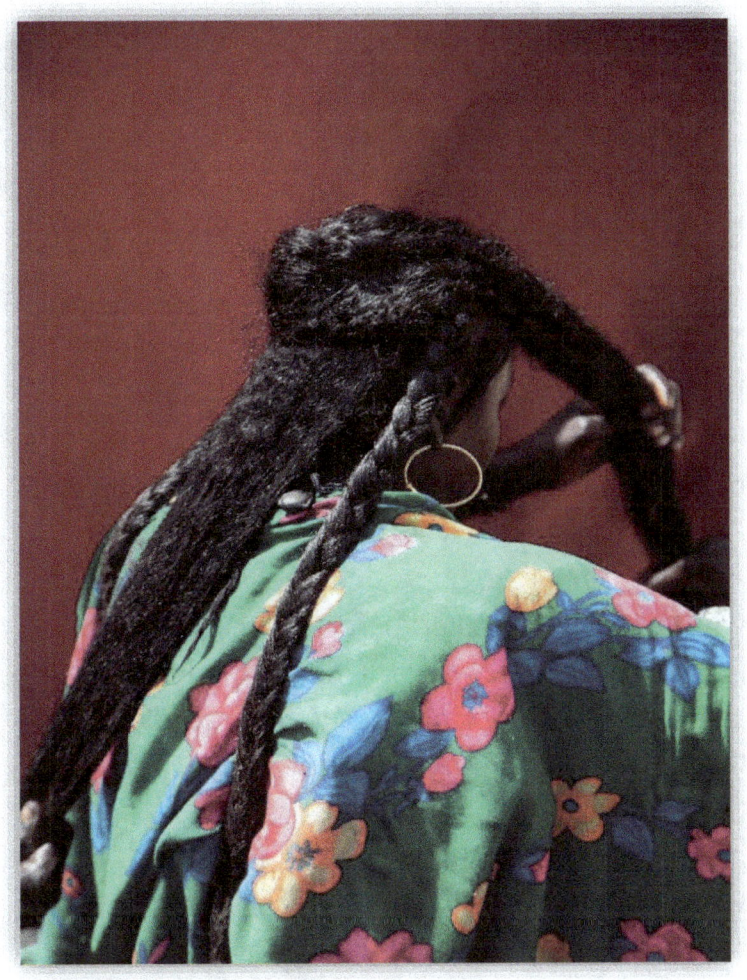

Basara Women in Chad

The Basara Women used Chebe powder, a shrub in Chad, to grow their hair. The Women believed Chébé was a gift God left up in the mountain to bring down the hair to great lengths. This Chebe is used now in the Billion-dollar Hair Industry in hair growth products.

In the Rocky Mountains of Chad's Guéra region, a native plant with rust-hued flower buds called croton gratissimus, known as Chébé, grows in droves. From February to April, its seeds are harvested, then sun-dried, winnowed, and roasted before they are blended into a fine silky powder. "Chébé powder is like a cooking recipe," says Salwa Petersen of Chad's Gorane (Dazagarè) tribe with a smile. "Everyone has their own way of doing it." To prepare the treatment before application, a woman will set out three bowls, one containing water, the second with Chébé powder, and the third with a mix of oils and butter, typically shea butter and sesame oil, says Petersen. Then, between alternating layers of water and a blend of oils and butter, she will spread the

Chébé powder through sections of a loved one's hair—generously, from roots to tips, for maximum moisture—while meticulously braiding the hair into long plaits that trail all the way down the back. "The traditional Chébé powder ritual is an extremely long, time-consuming, and labor-intensive process," says Petersen. "You must put aside at least an entire day if you want to follow all the steps."

Valenti, Lauren. "How the Nomadic Women of Chad Are Keeping the Ancient Hair-Care Ritual of Chébé Alive." Vogue, 8 Mar. 2022, https://www.vogue.com/article/chebe-hair-ritual-chad.

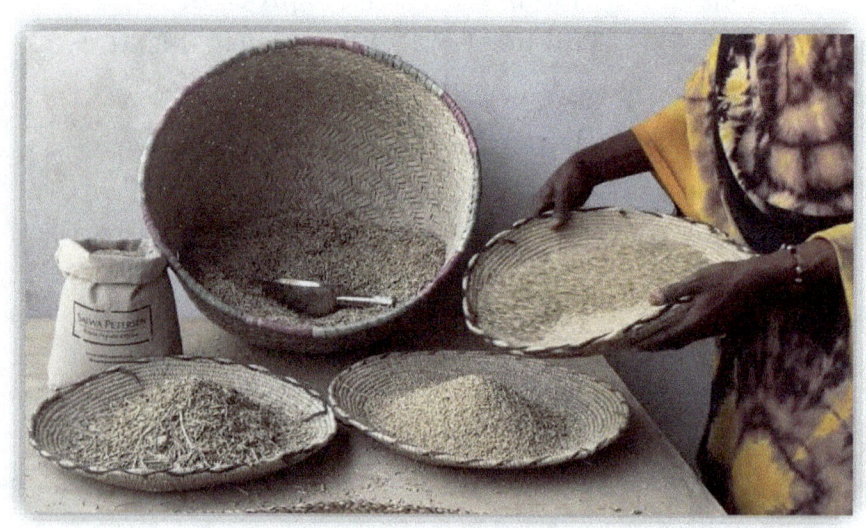

The Chebe seeds being winnowed to remove impurities

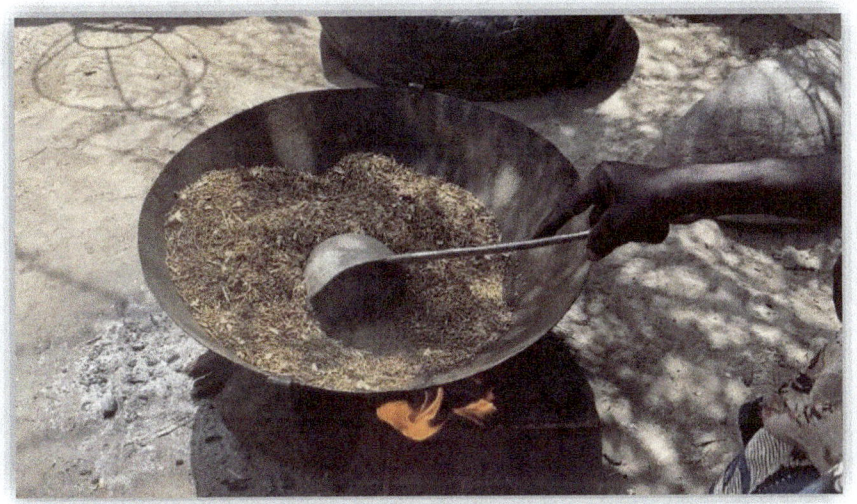

Chebe seeds are grilled and then pounded with a wooden
pestle and mortar into a silky fine powder.

Hair Types in Africa

Hair colors and textures vary throughout Africa. Hair varies from thin to thick and nearly straight to softly curling (e.g., the Ashanti) to tight curls (e.g., the Mandingo). Scientists 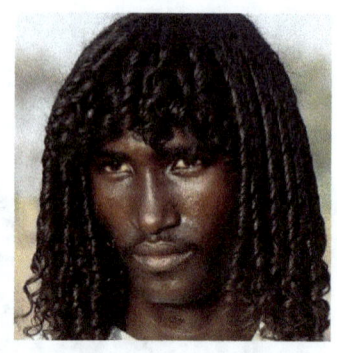 believe that the dense, curling hair texture most typical in Africa helps to shield the head from strong sunlight. About 75 percent of the dark-skinned people on the continent have hair labeled "kinky," while 15 percent have curly hair.

Curly hair is found among Ethiopians, Nubians, Somalians, and others. Straight or wavy hair on black Africans is most often found in very humid regions and in forested areas of the Sahara and Sudan.

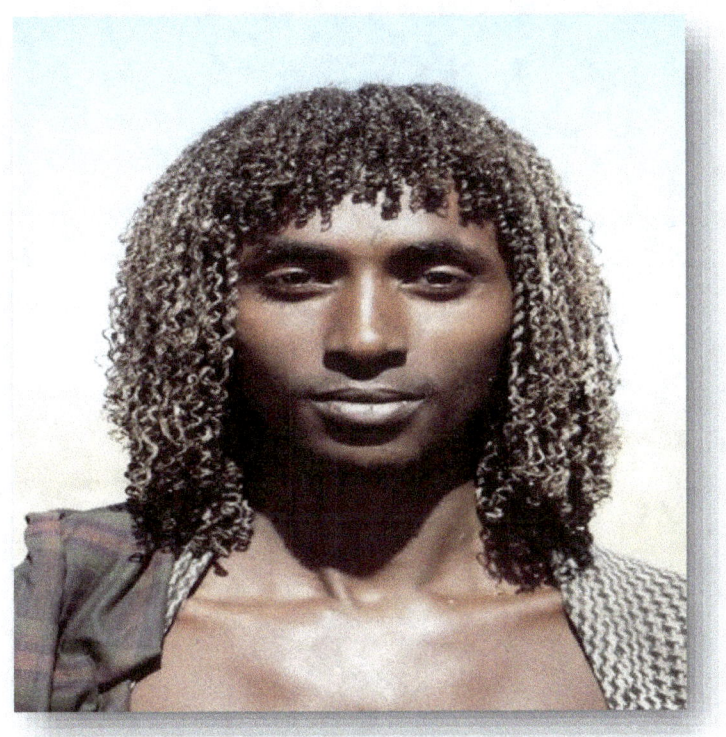

Beja man from Northeast Sudan

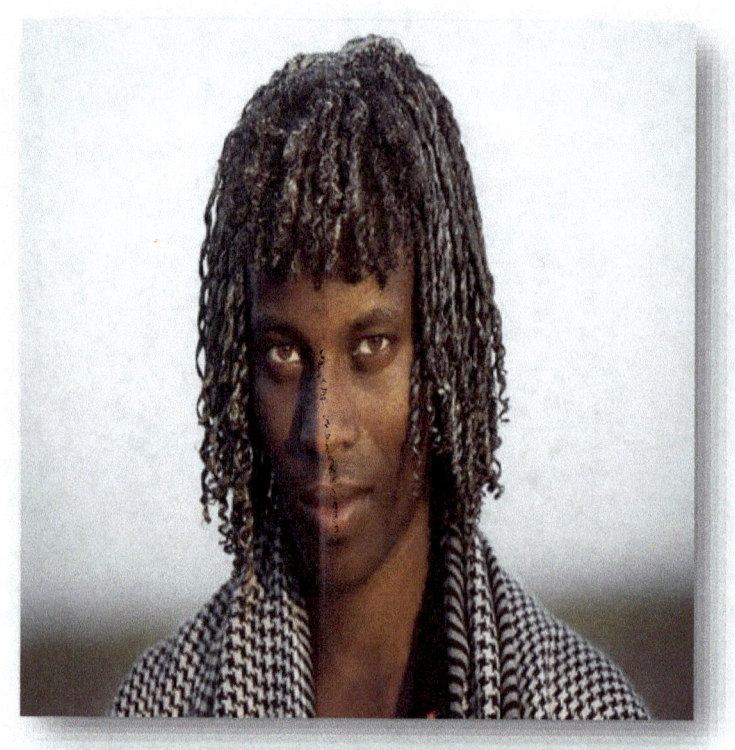

Afar man of Ethiopia and Djibouti

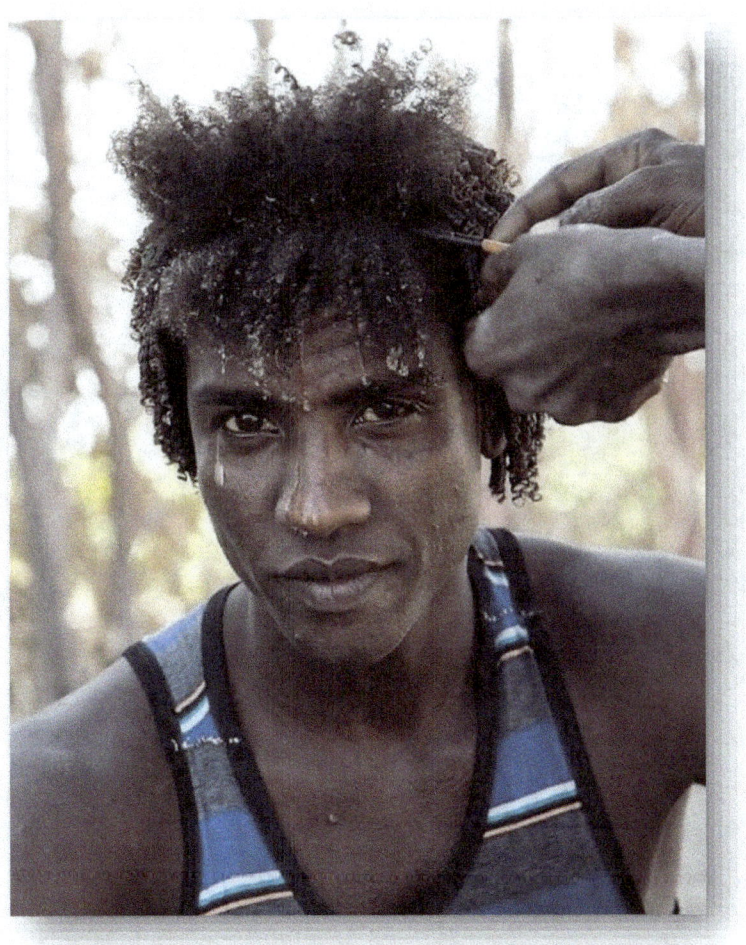

Afar man getting a traditional hairstyle

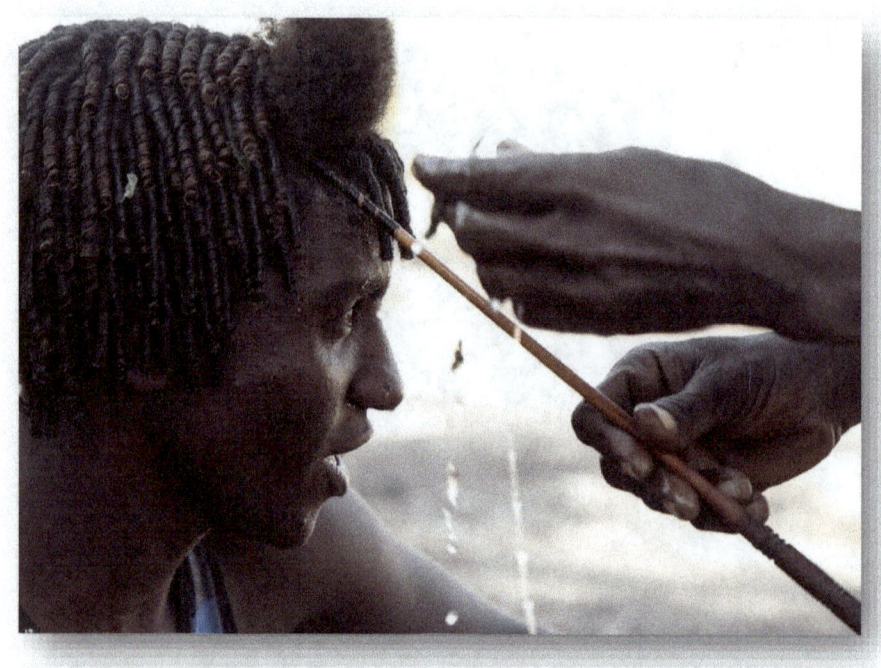

Afar man getting a traditional hairstyle

CHAPTER SIX

Nature Hair Care Products in Africa

Nature Hair Care Products in Africa

I know you, the reader, have been wondering did our brothers in sisters in Africa use any type of products for their and, if so, what were they using to shampoo, moisture, dye, curl, and straighten their hair and yes, I said straighten their hair and, I'll talk about that later in this chapter. Things we are doing right now to style and color our hair were done centuries ago, but I know it is hard for some of us to believe that because we have been conditioned to think that our Ancestors were primitive.

Hair Care Natural Ingredients

- Shea Butter
- Plants
- Shrubs
- Chebe Powder
- Butter
- Natural Herbs
- Castor Oil
- Coal
- Goat Hair
- Ochre
- Ashes

- Cow Urine
- Water
- Honey
- Animals fat

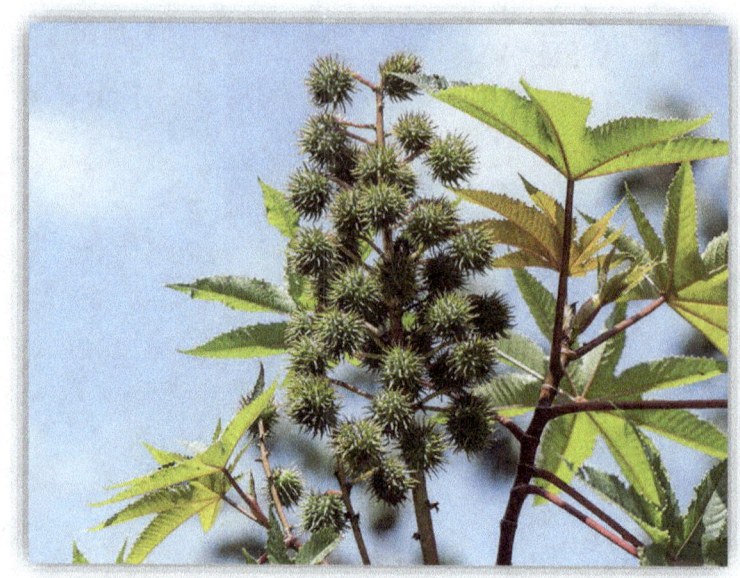

Castor Oil

Castor oil is a multipurpose vegetable oil that people have used for thousands of years. It's made by extracting oil from the seeds of the Ricinus communis plant. These seeds, known as castor beans, contain a toxic enzyme called ricin.

Arsian GG, et al. (2011). An examination of the effect of castor oil packs on constipation in the elderly.ncbi.nlm.nih.gov/pubmed/21168117

Castor oil plants native to Africa and India, castor oil plant, is a large flowering shrub with seeds that are poisonous to both humans and animals.

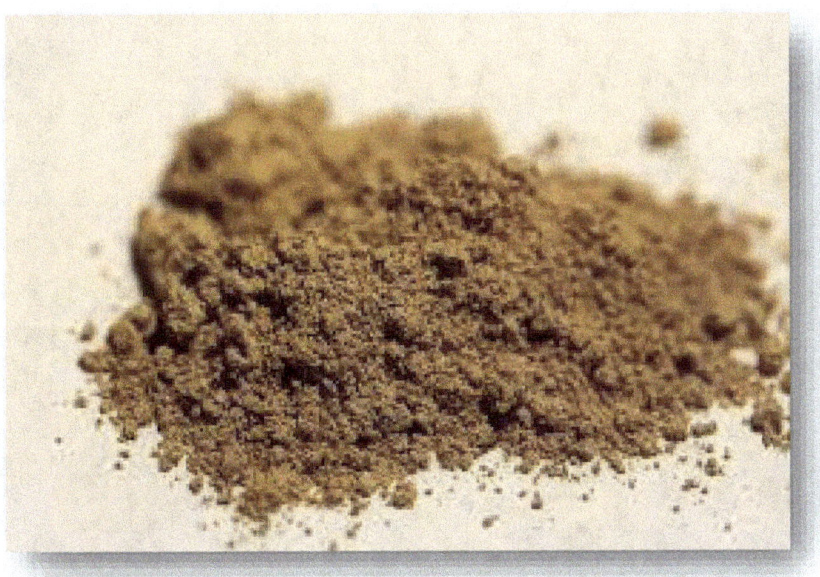

Orche

Ochre is a natural clay earth pigment, a mixture of ferric oxide and varying amounts of clay and sand. It ranges in color from yellow to deep orange or brown. It is also the name of the colors produced by this pigment, especially a light brownish-yellow. A variant of ochre containing a large amount of hematite, or dehydrated iron oxide, has a reddish tint known as "red ochre."

Ocher. American Heritage Dictionary. 1969.

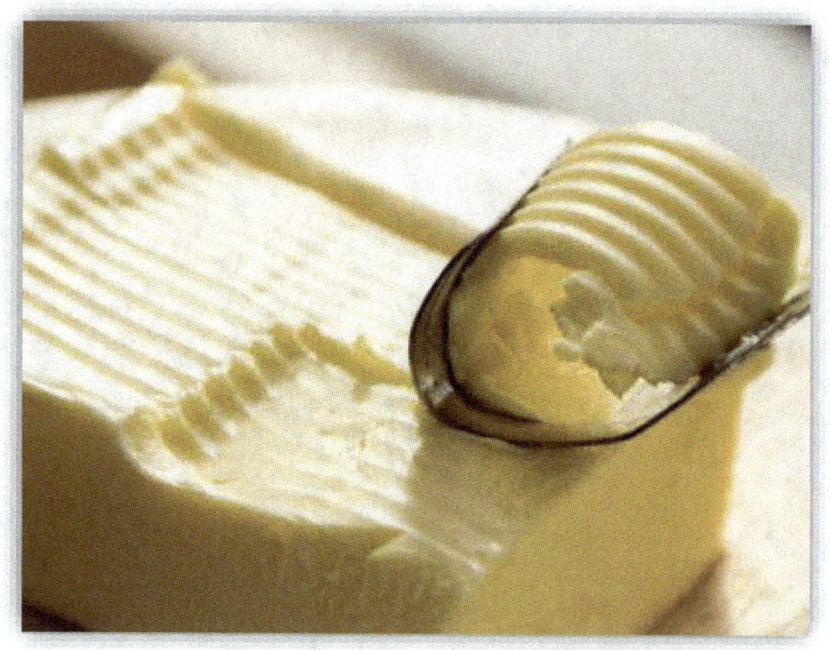

Butter

Butter is a dairy product made from the fat and protein components of churned cream. It is a semi-solid emulsion at room temperature, consisting of approximately 80% butterfat. It is used at room temperature as a spread, melted as a condiment, and used as a fat in baking, sauce-making, pan frying, and other cooking procedures.

Most frequently made from cow's milk, butter can also be manufactured from the milk of other mammals, including sheep, goats, buffalo, and yaks.

Institute of Medicine. Committee on Strategies to Reduce Sodium Intake; Henney, Jane E.; Taylor, Christine Lewis; Boon, Caitlin S. (2010). "4: Preservation and Physical Property Roles of Sodium in Foods"

Khosrova traces butter's beginning back to ancient Africa, in 8000 B.C., when a herder making a journey with a sheepskin container of milk strapped to the back of one of his sheep found that the warm sheep's milk, jostled in travel, had curdled into something delicious.

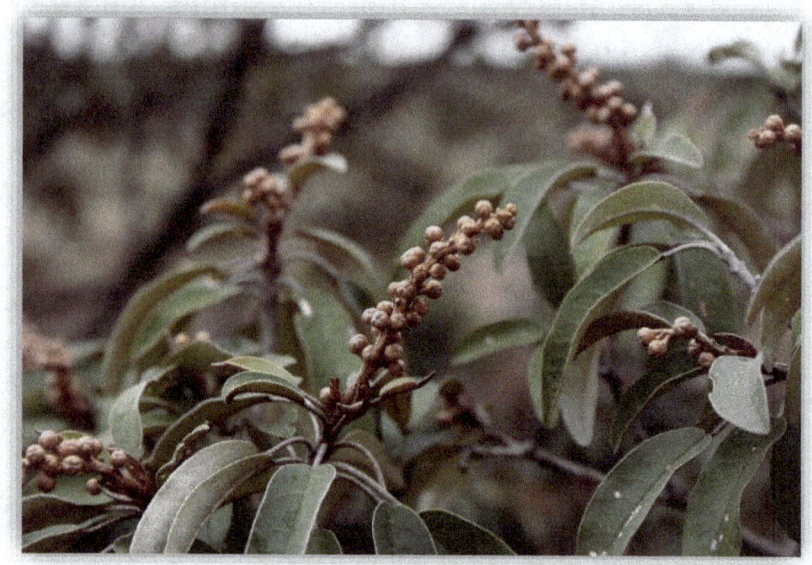

Chebe

The scientific name of the plant, which they refer to as 'Chebe,' is called Croton Zambesicus (Also known as Lavender Croton). It is a shrub, and it is grown all over Africa, primarily in West Africa, mainly Ghana, Nigeria, Gambia, Chad, and Burkina Faso.

Bozdogan, Cihangir. "Chebe Powder from Chad for Natural Hair Growth: 4C Natural Afro Hair." Jostylin, https://jostylin.com/chebe-powder-for-natural-hair-growth.

In West Africa, Lavender Croton is used not only for hair care but to treat various ailments, including dropsy, indigestion, uterine disorder, and its leaves are used to make perfumes.

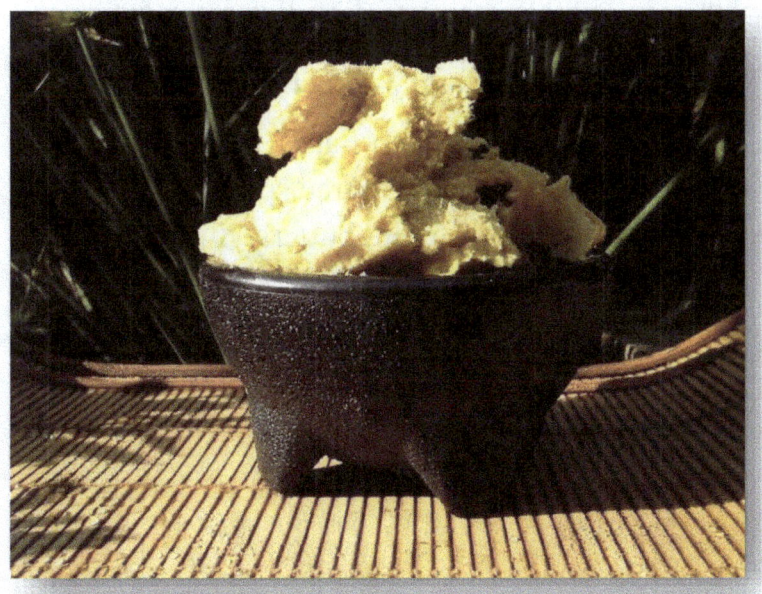

Shea Butter

Shea butter is a fat extracted from the nut of the African shea tree (Vitellaria paradoxaIt is ivory in color when raw and commonly dyed yellow with borututu root or palm oil. It is widely used in cosmetics as a moisturizer, salve, or lotion. Shea butter is edible and is used in food preparation in some African countries. Occasionally, shea butter is mixed with other oils as a substitute for cocoa butter, although the taste is noticeably different.

Alfred Thomas (2002). "Fats and Fatty Oils." Ullmann's Encyclopedia of Industrial Chemistry. Weinheim: Wiley-VCH

There are two tree sub-species that yield shea butter nuts. The first is Vitellaria Paradoxa from West Africa (Ghana and Nigeria). The second is Vitellaria Nilotica from East Africa (Uganda). Each of the two tree species produces slightly different butters. Shea Butter from West Africa is more dense and clay-like. While the shea produced in East Africa is creamier. Other than that, both butters are comparable in quality and nutrient content.

Mercy et al. "Shea Butter Origins: Where Does Shea Butter Come from?" Better Shea Butter Shea Butter Origins Where Does Shea Butter Come From Comments, 6 May 2019, https://bettersheabutter.com/where-does-shea-butter-come-from

Shea butter is mainly used in the cosmetics industry for skin- and hair-related products (lip gloss, skin moisturizer creams and emulsions, and hair conditioners for dry and brittle hair.

Soap makers and massage oil manufacturers also use it, typically in small amounts, because it has plenty of unsaponifiable, and higher amounts result in softer soaps that have less cleaning abilities.

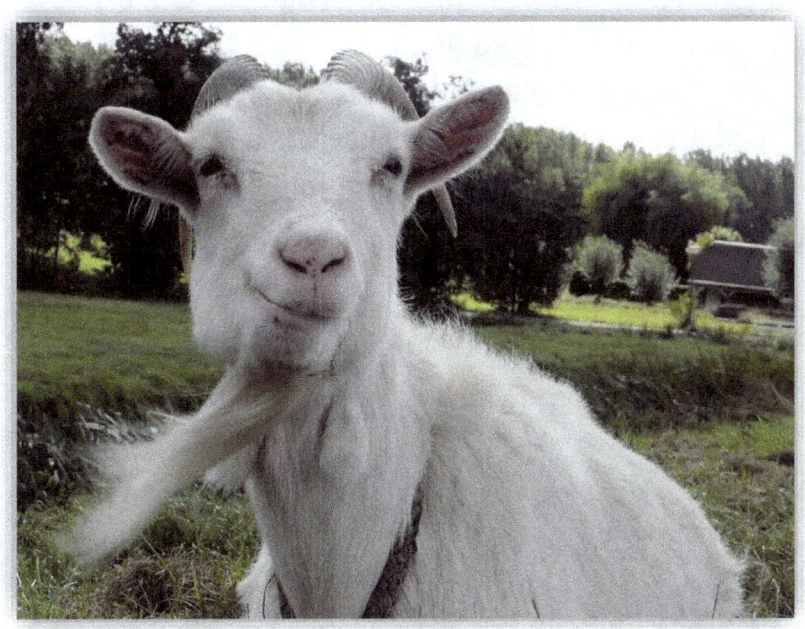

Goat

goat, any ruminant and hollow-horned mammal belonging to the genus Capra. Related to the sheep, the goat is lighter in build, has horns that arch backward, a short tail, and straighter hair. Male goats, called bucks or belly's, usually have a beard. Females are called does, or nannys, and immature goats are called kids. Wild goats include the ibex and markhor.

"Goat Definition & Meaning." Merriam-Webster, Merriam-Webster, https://www.merriam-webster.com/dictionary/goat.

I listed a few things our brothers and sisters use in nature as hair care products, and I know you are saying goat hair. Yeah, I mention goat hair in chapter 3. Goat hair was used as an extension, so extensions is nothing new. When the Himba women dreadlocked their hair, they used a mixture of ground ochre, butter, and goat hair for extensions.

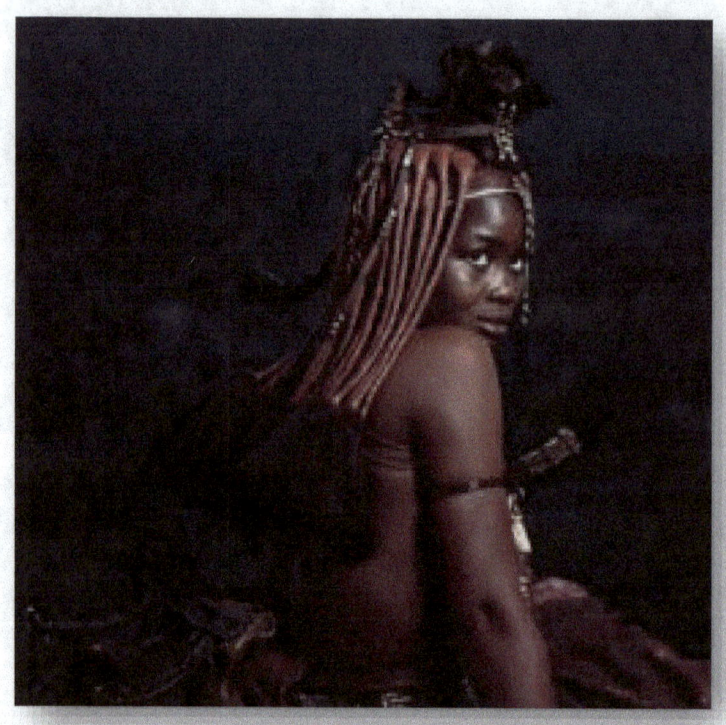

The red color in their hair is Ochre, which was used to dye their hair, and we see this use across Africa. The Samburu warrior uses ochred in their hair to dye it red. A mixture of cow's urine and ashes is often rubbed into the hair first to help straighten it. The wooden headrest is also used as a pillow at night.

Ashes were one of the natural hair care ingredients I listed early in this chapter, and Africans straighten their hair with ashes and cow urine. I do not want to hear we didn't straighten our hair centuries ago. The method of straightening hair was used to style the hair, particularly with braids.

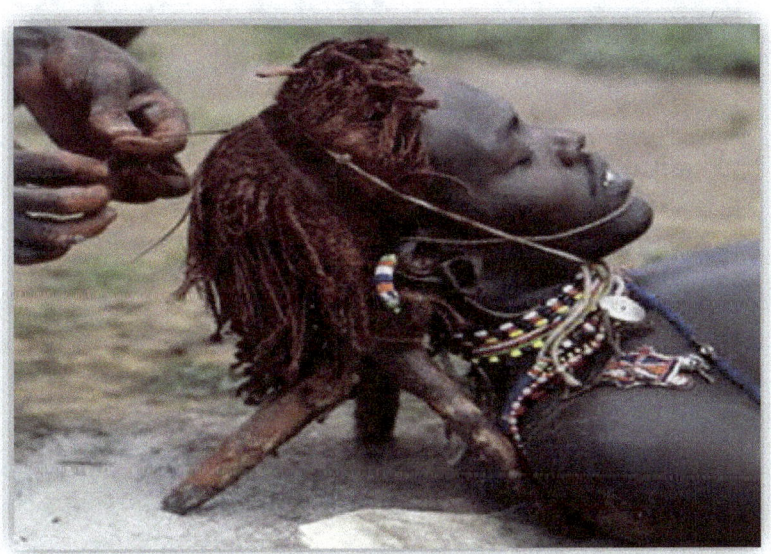

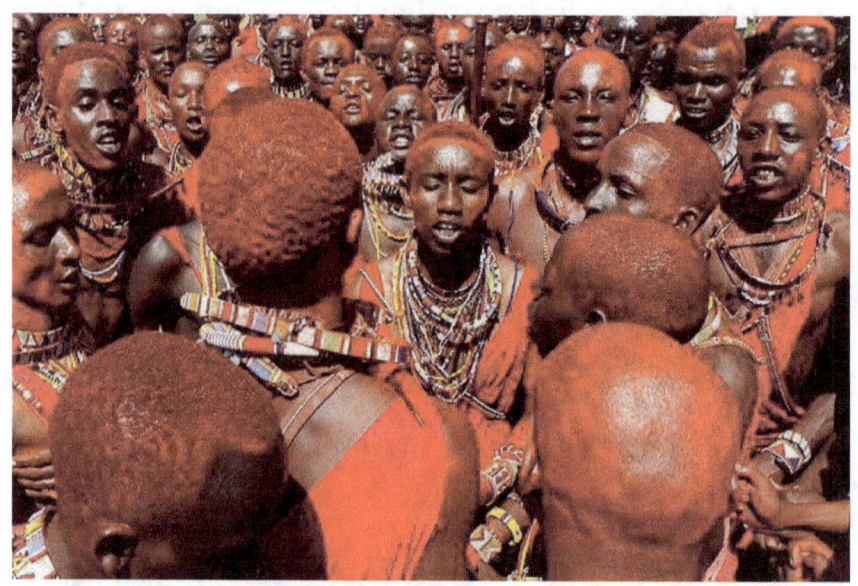

Massai Boys have red ochre hair, and Massai warrior's braided hair is dyed red, and the Massai people are also native to Kenya.

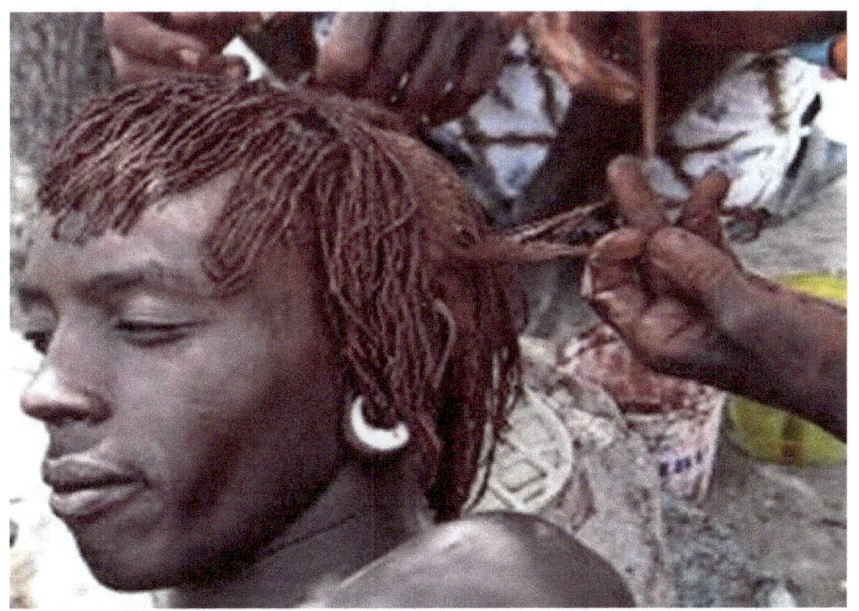

Maasai man getting his hair dyed

Castor Oil, Egypt

In ancient Egypt, hair symbolized beauty, wealth, status, and fertility. Most Egyptians used castor oil for their hair to maintain the growth and strength of their natural hair due to its nourishing properties. The oil is massaged into the hair and scalp, and then a hot wrap is put over it. This enables the vitamins and fatty acids in the concentrated castor oil to penetrate deeply into the scalp and hair follicles. Recently, castor oil has become popular among beauticians and natural hair enthusiasts who want to achieve the perfect natural hair.

Botchwey, Adom Tabbey. Ancient African Hair Care Products That Worked Wonders. Face2Face Africa , n.d..

Butter, Ethiopia

Clarified butter (also known as Niter kibbeh) has been used by the people of the Afar tribe in Ethiopia as a hair care product for centuries. To make this, butter is simmered for a length of time, allowing milk fat or solids to separate and the water to evaporate, leaving behind a distinctive fat rich in essential fatty acids, as well as, some fat-soluble vitamins, which are needed for multiple physiological functions in the body.

Botchwey, Adom Tabbey. Ancient African Hair Care Products That Worked Wonders. Face2Face Africa, n.d..

Our brothers and sisters on the continent of Africa drew from nature to get the ingredients for their hair care products. Ochre, butter, and water were used a lot in mixing up their products. When I mention products, I know you might think of bottled products with labels and dollar amounts attached, but they weren't going from community to community, selling them to make a profit.

Now I mention ochre, butter, and water, and with high or very elaborate hairstyles, they would use ochre and animal fat as a holding spray to make the hairstyle last longer.

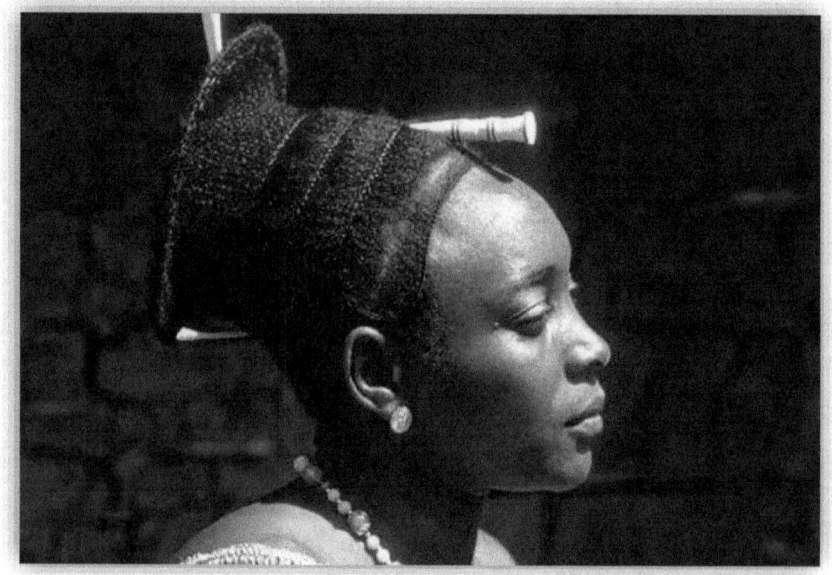

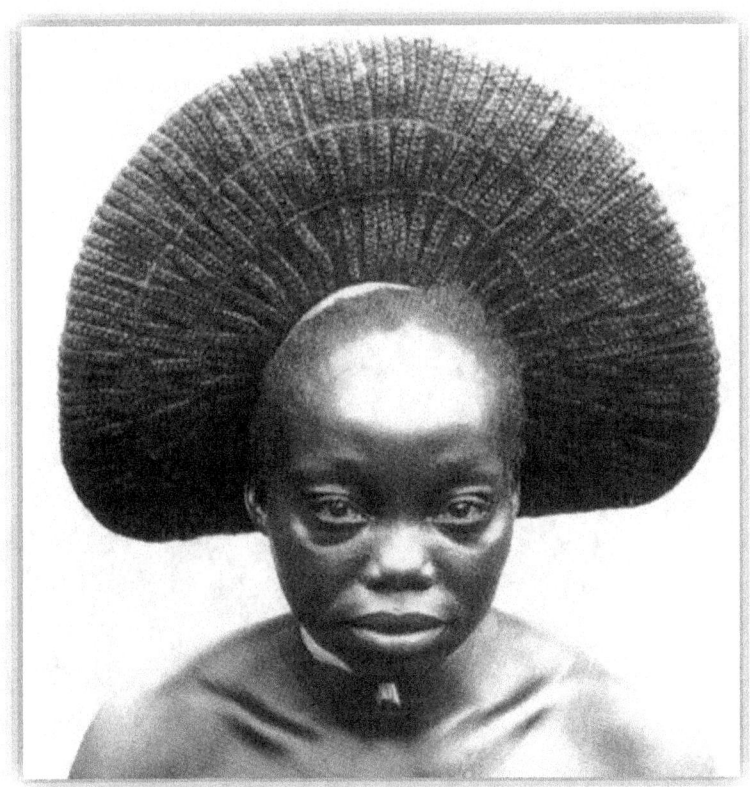

Nasara, one of the wives of Akenge, with typical fan-shaped style of the Zande, Democratic Republic of Congo.

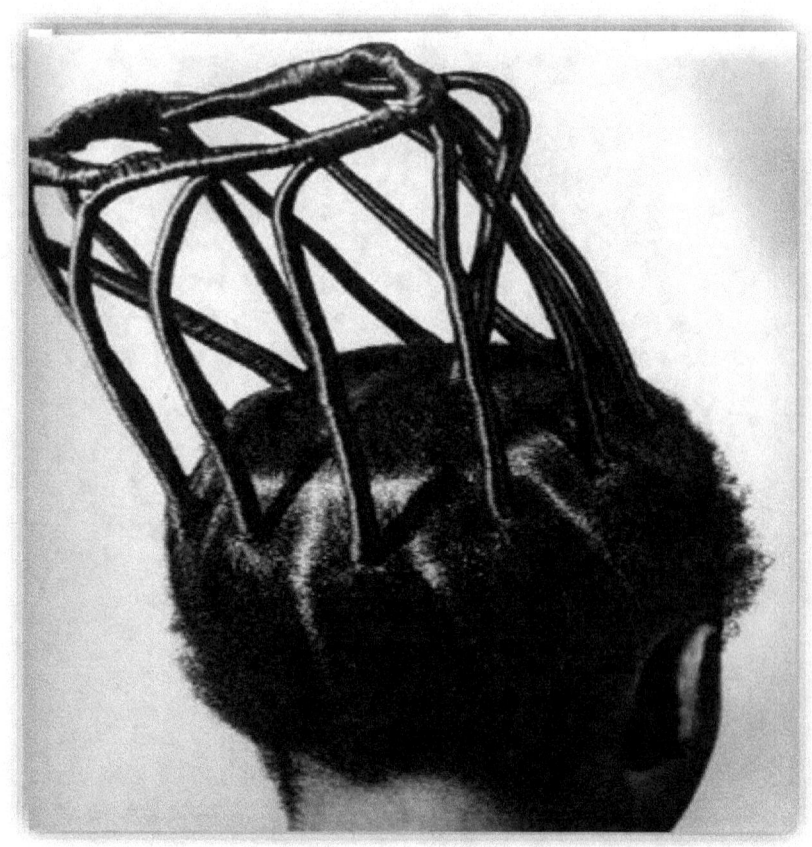

Hairstyles That Ascend and Aspire, in Nigeria

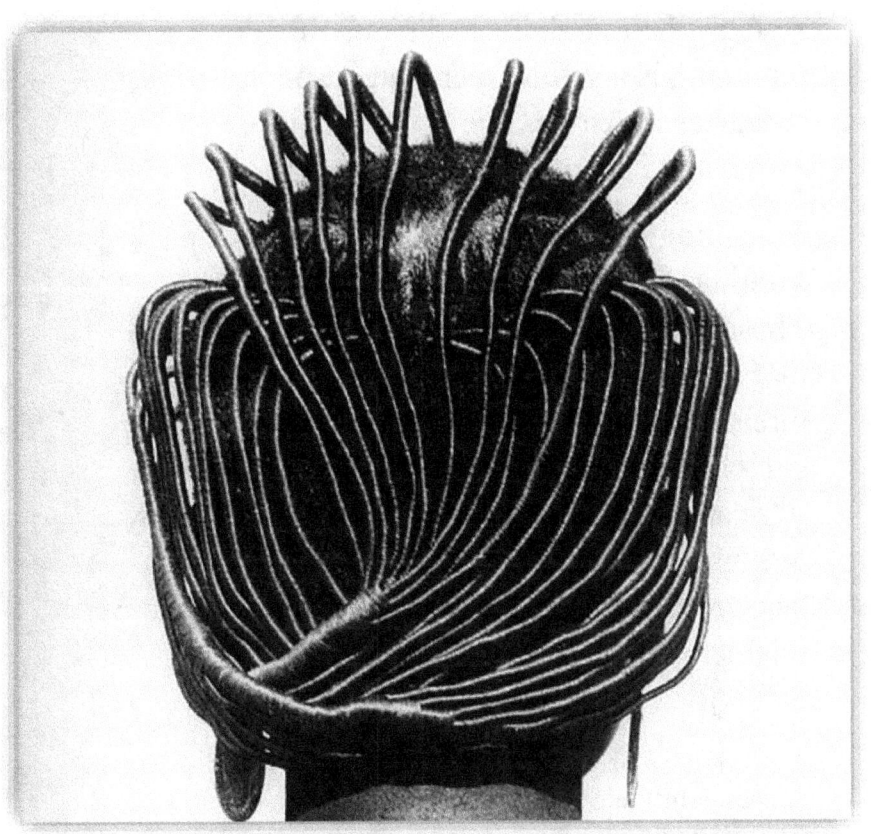

Hairstyles That Ascend and Aspire in Nigeria

The last two elaborate hairstyles on pages 126 and 127 they use a technique of threading to style the hair, and this technique of hair threading is a styling technique used in various countries in Africa. It is known to have originated in central and western Africa.

Threading of the hair helped in creating hair sculptural designs with complex techniques. These designs created three-dimensional forms that are aesthetically pleasing. Though most threaded styles had a purpose, they also helped stretch the hair to aid healthy growth (Zakaria). African natural hair, which is also called nappy or kinky hair, is usually thick and hard. The hair grows upwards and is stiffened and made pliable by wrapping selected sections of the hair with a thread.

Akorli, Rudith Senam Abla, "Reveal" (2014). Thesis. Rochester Institute of Technology.

There that word nappy goes again, and I hate that word, and I wish we would eradicate that word from our minds. Rudith Senam Abla Akorli went on to state in her thesis "Reveal" When threading, black wrapping wool, nylon, or cotton threads were gradually wrapped or knotted evenly and sometimes unevenly around the hair to create the desired effect. Threaded hair was sometimes coiled and bent into geometric, symmetrical, or asymmetrical shapes on top of the crown ("The Art of air Threading").

I was googling for more African hairstyle's images to use for the book cover for this book, possibly. I ran across an article from an interview with a young West African woman named Laetitia Ky. I began to look at her geometric, symmetrical hairstyles, and I was like, wow. After looking at the few pictures in the article, I read the interview transcripts to see what inspired her to use her hair as beautiful art pieces. Her inspiration came from archival photographs of all African women's hairstyles. Now from those pictures, she began these sculptures of beautiful hair art. After reading the article, I found out she had an Instagram page, and I immediately went to her page to see if she had more images of sculpture hairstyles which she called "Ky Concepts." I began to scroll her page, and she had tons of Ky Concepts on there.

Ky hairstyle sculptures are created from wire, thread, and her dreadlocks lengthened with weaves into her natural hair. Laetitia Ky's sculptured hair has become more political, and now she uses her platform on social media to raise awareness.

A few paragraphs back, I mentioned threaded hair was sometimes coiled and bent into **geometric**, **symmetric**, or **asymmetrica**l shapes on top of the crown (The art of hair threading.) On the next few pages is Laetitia Ky, Ky Concepts of her sculptured geometric, symmetrical hairstyles.

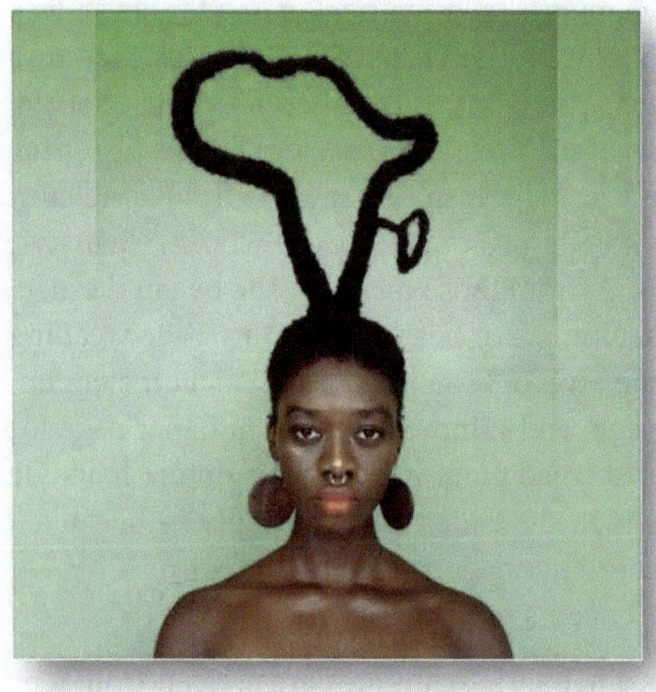

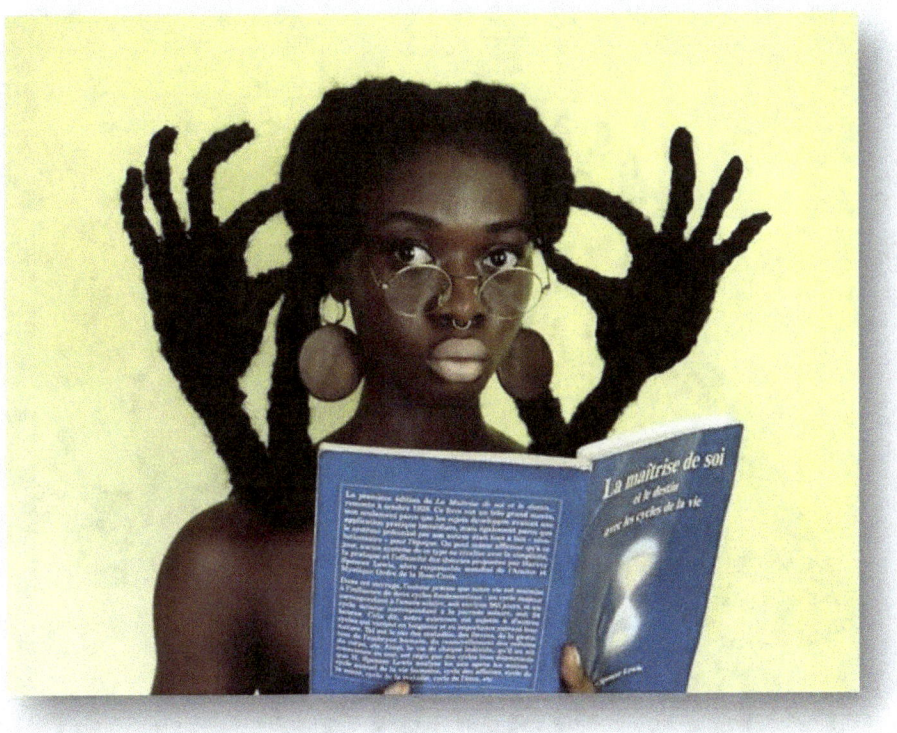

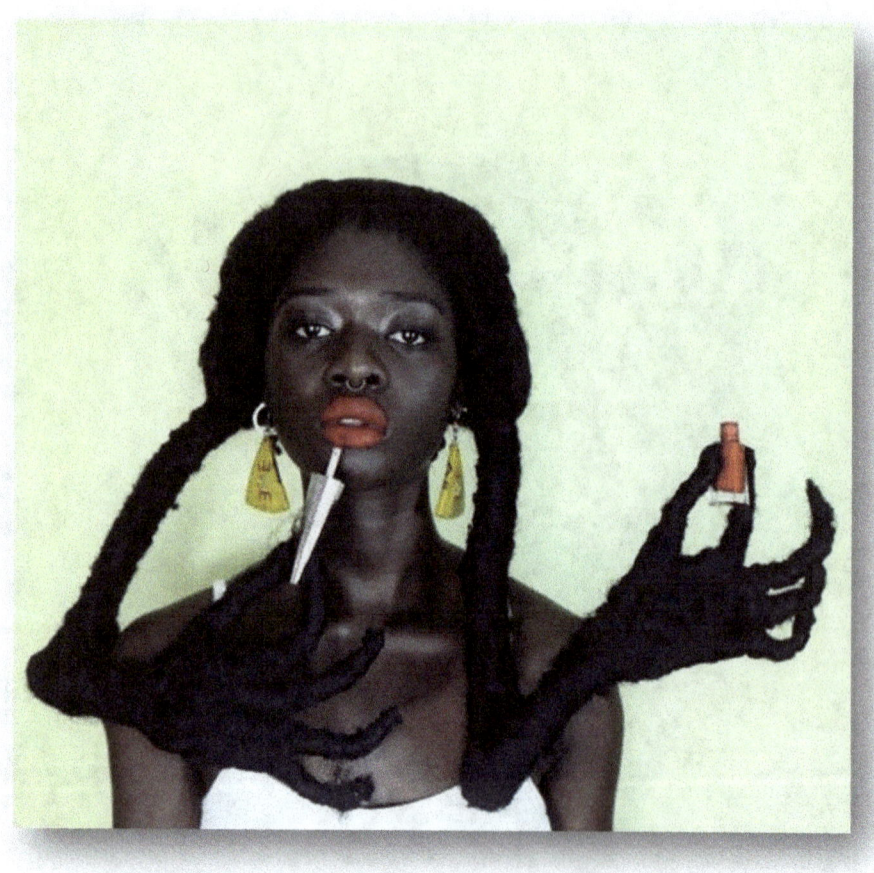

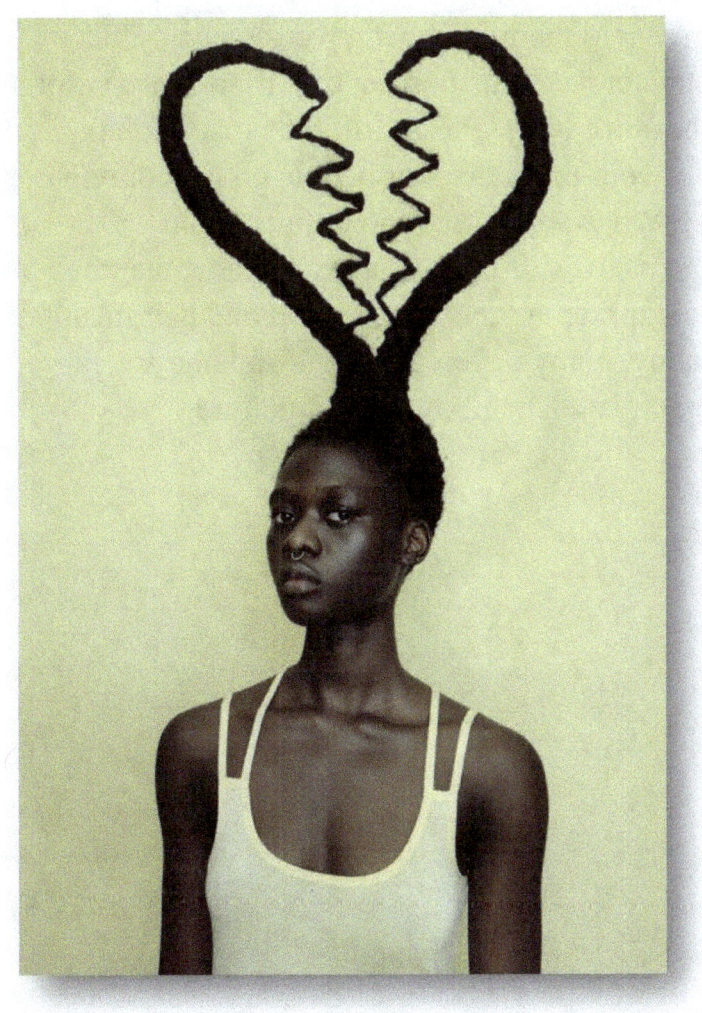

From braiding, threading, combing, twisting, locing, and straightening their hair, we have to give it to them; they were very stylish. This chapter ends this portion of Africa's hair before the slave trade. Please kill the noise and take out your mind that our people on the continent of Africa were dirty and didn't groom themselves. It is a lie, and you know that they took pride in their appearance, and hair meant many, many different things, and hair was an essential element in African culture.

CHAPTER SEVEN

What Hair Looks Like After Slavery

What Hair Looks Like After Slavery

Trans-Atlantic Slave Trade

The Trans-Atlantic Slave Trade by the Europeans changes everything for Central and West Africans. Let's briefly talk about the Trans-Atlantic Slave Trade. The Portuguese and later the English, French, and Dutch got involved in enslaving Africans in large parts of West Africa; the Gulf of Guinea coast and the Congo River basin were significant areas of human exports to the Americas, mostly to sugar plantations in the Caribbean.

By the late 17th century, the so-called Triangle Trade developed. European ships loaded with guns, textiles, tobacco, and manufactured goods sailed to African slave ports and traded those goods for captives. European slave traders then took those Africans to the New World, where they were sold. With that money, the Europeans purchased staples such as sugar, tobacco, rum, and coffee, then sold for enormous profit back in Europe. That profit was often reinvested in other goods to be traded for captives back in Africa, and so on.

If you want more in-depth information on Trans-Atlantic Slave Trade, I recommend you read Hugh Thomas's book titled The Slave Trade: The Story of the Atlantic Slave Trade, 1440-1870. This is a thick book, ruffly 912 pages, and worth sacrificing some of your time to read. The book is almost the same price as a super-size combo from a fast-food restaurant.

Destroying the image of Africans hair

Europeans, who had long traded and communicated with Africans, knew the complexity and significance of Black hair. They were often struck by the various hairstyles that they saw within each community. In an effort to dehumanize and break the African spirit, Europeans shaved the heads of enslaved Africans upon arrival to the Americas. This was not merely a random act but a symbolic removal of African culture. The shaving of the hair represented a removal of any trace of African identity and further acted to dehumanize.

Johnson, Tabora A., and Teiahsha Bankhead. "Hair It Is: Examining the Experiences of Black Women with Natural Hair." Open Journal of Social Sciences, vol. 02, no. 01, 2014, pp. 86–100. https://doi.org/10.4236/jss.2014.21010.

Africans came to the Americas in bondage. Africans with cultural identities such as Wolof, Asantes, Fulanis, and Mandingos entered the slave ships, yet enslaved, unidentifiable people exited onto the shores of the Americas.

Without their combs, oils, and native hair recipes, Africans could not care for an essential part of themselves. Europeans deemed African hair unattractive and did not consider it to be hair; for them, it was considered the fur of animals and was referred to as wool or woolly. In an analysis of Africans' hair, a White anthropologist reported that the hair types ranged from peppercorn, tufted, and matted to woolly. He adds that the hair's "spirality appears to have produced the matted condition.

 It is not the result of accumulated dirt or anything of that sort, as might appear at first sight." This "spirality" refers to the unique nature of Black hair to spiral upwards naturally and form tightly dense coiled hair. However, instead of acknowledging its uniqueness, Black hair is described in pejorative terms. Words such as peppercorn, matted and woolly remain in the lexicon of people in the US, Africa, the Caribbean, and worldwide to describe Black hair. We observe that the descriptions that emerged in the 1800 and 1900s remain current irrespective of societal changes.

Johnson, Tabora A., and Teiahsha Bankhead. "Hair It Is: Examining the Experiences of Black Women with Natural Hair." Open Journal of Social Sciences, vol. 02, no. 01, 2014, pp. 86–100., https://doi.org/10.4236/jss.2014.21010.

The word matted came up a couple of times, and according to authors Ayana Byrd and Lori Tharps, the inhumane condition in which the slaves had to live, they had no time or energy to take care of their hair as they used to back home.

Plus, they did not have any of their African styling tools (such as combs) that they used to have back home; therefore, slaves had nothing to style their hair with. Therefore, their hair became matted. Since they did not know what to use to comb their hair, out of desperation, slaves started to detangle their hair with sheep fleece carding tools. Unfortunately, using these tools resulted in nasty scalp infections, hair breakage, and hair loss. As a result, women slaves started to wrap their hair with pieces of fabric, which started the history of headwraps in African American history. Headwraps were partly used to protect the hair but were also worn out of shame because of their depraved condition.

Byrd, Ayana D., and Lori L. Tharps. Hair Story: Untangling the Roots of Black Hair in America. St. Martin's Griffin, 2002.

The Slave master's wife didn't make it any easier on the women whose jobs were normal domestic work and would make the African women feel bad about their skin and hair and wouldn't let her in the house if her hair wasn't wrapped up.

The African woman's head-wrap (dhuku) holds a distinctive position in the history of African dress both for its longevity and for its potent signification. It endured the travail of colonialism and never passed out of fashion. The dhuku represents far more than a piece of fabric wound around the head.

Griebel, Helen Bradley. The African American Woman's Headwrap: Unwinding the Symbols, http://char.txa.cornell.edu/Griebel.htm.

This distinct cloth head covering has been called variously 'head rag,' 'head-tie,' 'head handkerchief,' 'turban,' or 'head-wrap.' The head wrap usually completely covers the hair, being held in place by tying the ends into knots close to the skull. As a form of apparel in Zimbabwe, the head wrap has been exclusive to women of African descent.

The head wrap originated in sub-Saharan Africa and served similar functions for African and African American women. In style, the African American woman's head wrap exhibits the features of sub-Saharan aesthetics and worldview. In the United States, however, the head wrap acquired a paradox of meaning not customary on the ancestral continent.

Griebel, Helen Bradley. The African American Woman's Headwrap: Unwinding the Symbols, http://char.txa.cornell.edu/Griebel.htm.

The Head Wrap was a badge of slavery and was forced on their heads before entering the plantation home. Let me say this on some plantations in other counties or states, African women's working indoors and more closely to their masters had to be neat, so they wore wigs and not head wraps. Some African women made a way to make their hair resemble as much as possible to their master's straight hair because that was the beauty standard.

Having straight hair was not only a synonym for beauty but also a synonym for prosperity. Slaves of mixed race, who often had looser curls pattern and thinner features, were often privileged. Having those features was associated with freedom because many mixed-race slaves were free.

Slaves attempted to achieve this look, hoping it would convince their slave masters that they deserved freedom.

Byrd, Ayana D., and Lori L. Tharps. Hair Story: Untangling the Roots of Black Hair in America. St. Martin's Griffin, 2002.

In the last chapter, I talk about the things they grab from nature to make their hair care products for their hair. Now they had to make do with whatever they could get access to wash, condition, and moisturize their hair. They use bacon fat, butter, and kerosene. Kerosene is a light fuel oil obtained by distilling petroleum, mainly used in jet engines and domestic heaters and lamps and as a cleaning solvent. I would have been scared to wash my hair with kerosene.

Tignon Laws

The tignon law (also known as the chignon law) was a 1786 law enacted by the Spanish Governor of Louisiana Esteban Rodríguez Miró that forced black women to wear a tignon headscarf. The law was intended to halt plaçage unions and tie freed black women to those who were enslaved, but the women who followed the law have been described as turning the headdress into a "mark of distinction.

Clinton, Catherine; Gillespie, Michele (1997-06-26). The Devil's Lane: Sex and Race in the Early South. Oxford University Press. p. 238

It was believed that black women exhibited unacceptable behaviors, including the hairstyles they wore. These hairstyles drew the attention of white men.

Black women were, apparently, wearing their hair in such lovely ways, adding jewels and feathers to their high hairdos and walking around with such beauty and pride that it was obscuring their status. This disrupted the social stability of white women. Therefore, the law was introduced to minimize a black woman's beauty. In many societies, white women would cut off a black woman's hair as they felt that her hair 'confused white men.

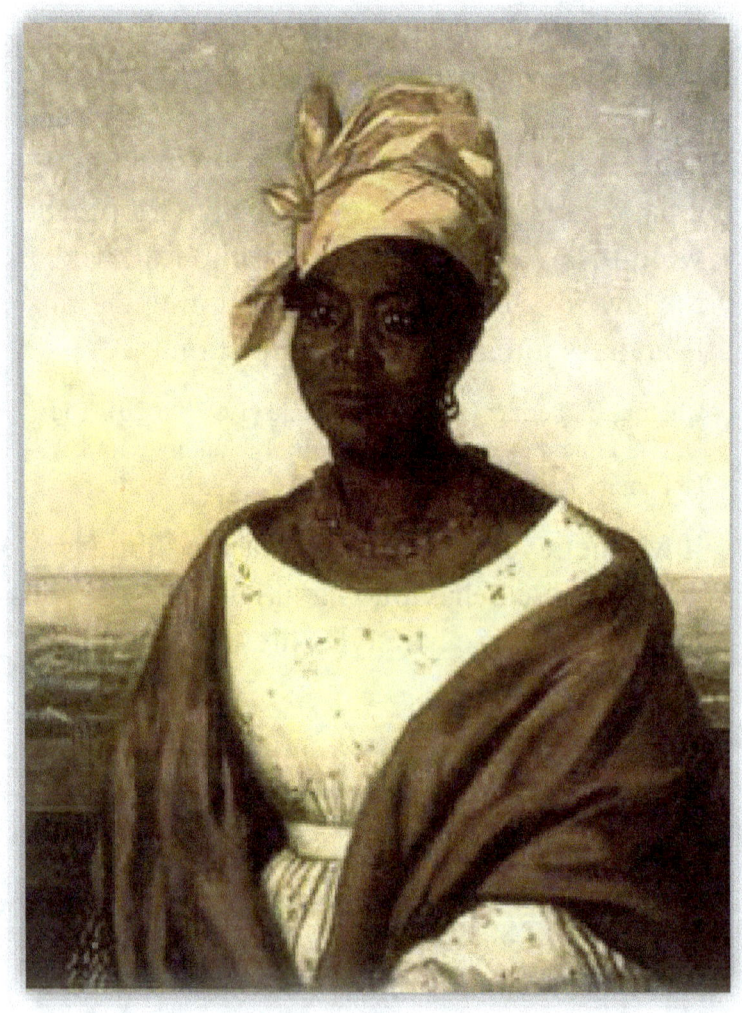

Free Woman of Color in Tignon

I want to talk about the durag for a moment since we are discussing head rag,' 'head-tie,' 'head handkerchief,' or 'head-wrap.'

What Is a Durag?

It's a piece of cloth or a wave cap that black people wear around the head. It's worn to accelerate the waves' development, dreadlocks, and braids in the hair. These are also used to keep the wave patterns in place while sleeping. This cloth could be made of silk, velvet, and various types of fabrics.

Safi, Raheem. The History of Durags. 2022.

One of the earliest published records of the durag was in the June 1966 Akron Beacon Journal, then spelled "Do Rag." It was described as "a cloth band worn around the forehead as a sweatband to keep hair in place." They had evolved from the 19th century when slave women used head wraps to keep their hair up and out of the way during labor. Companies like So Many Waves were credited for selling their version of the durag in the late 1970s, calling theirs the "Tie-down." It became a necessary tool for Black men to train their curl patterns or lock down hairstyles during sleep.

The durag remained exclusively functional until the 1990s, when it became a symbol of inner-city Black culture. Years before the fashion industry noticed it had become fashionable in the streets. The durag transitioned from a haircare item into a legit style accessory, most notably popularized by hip-hop and reflected on the heads of men and boys throughout the country.

Singleton, Saleam. "The History of the Durag and How It Became a Cultural Symbol of Pride." Byrdie, Byrdie, 15 Sept. 2022, https://www.byrdie.com/history-of-durag-4798963.

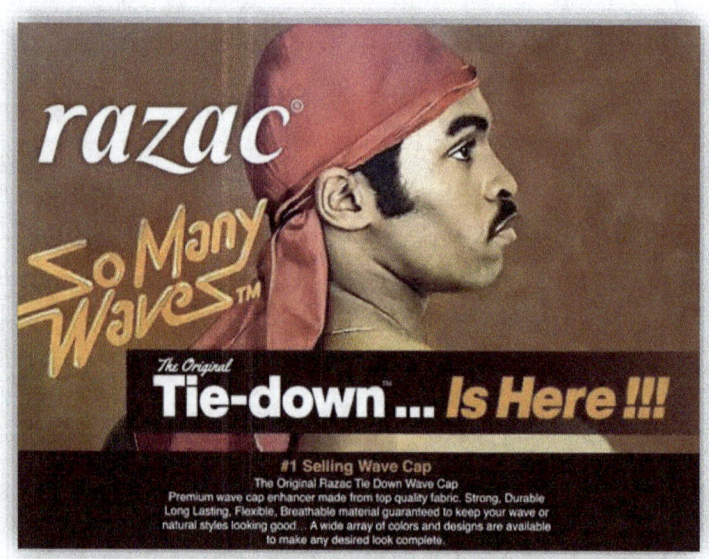

In the 2000s, they lost their public popularity in various areas, but not in all. Due to rappers like A$AP Ferg, 50 Cent, Meek Mill, and various other celebrities and the popularity of waves, these durags regained their status. Nowadays, it's worn by many celebrities of both genders as a fashion statement. They come in different colors and fabrics and use by people of all ages of both genders.

Who Created Them?

Well, there is no exact history about who created them, but the trend of using a scarf to keep the hairstyle in place leaped forward back in the 70s. However, Darren Dowdy, the president of So Many Waves, claims his dad, William J. Dowdy, invented Durag as a crucial part of the hair grooming kit. He called durag a tie-down, so they were first sold in 1979.

Darren Dowdy further added that his father wanted to keep the hair in place, and the idea was to keep a natural, tightly coiled hair structure in its place. This tie-down is used to protect hair patterns.

Why Was It Created?

Thanks to the way our hair grows out but keeping them down and free from frizzing could be challenging. To keep 360 waves in place, it's necessary for hair to lay down and stays down, and that's why the durag was invented. These can sit tight on the head and help make the hair flat.

Similarly, braids can have the same issue that 360 waves do, frizzy over time. Durags were invented to work for keeping braids together, especially while sleeping. In simple words, durags were invented to keep hairstyles intact.

Safi, Raheem. The History of Durags. 2022.

Cornrows

Cornrows were the go hairstyle in slavery. Cornrows were not a hairstyle created in slavery, but if you made it this far in the book, you already know that. This hairstyle was manageable on the plantation and could last for a couple of weeks. I have read a few articles saying these tight braids that we call cornrows were a small act of rebellion and resistance to keep their heritage close to them. I also came across in my reading that enslaved Africans also used cornrows to transfer and create maps to leave plantations and the home of their captors. This act of using hair as a tool for resistance is said to have been evident across South America.

It is most documented in Colombia, where Benkos Bioho, a King captured from Africa by the Portuguese who escaped slavery, built San Basilio de Palenque, a village in Northern Colombia, around the 17th century. Bioho created his own language as well as intelligence network and came up with the idea to have women create maps and deliver messages through their cornrows.

I don't know if they used cornrows as maps to escape the plantation. I need to see more evidence of this, and I thought I would get more reading about Benkos Bioho, a maroon leader who also built a village that was meant to be a refuge for escaped slaves and help them get back on their feet.

Again, it could have been possible to create a map using cornrow designs because I know they use quilts with hidden messages and different designs on the quilts as a map to escape to a safe haven, such as churches that would hide and keep them safe after escaping the plantation.

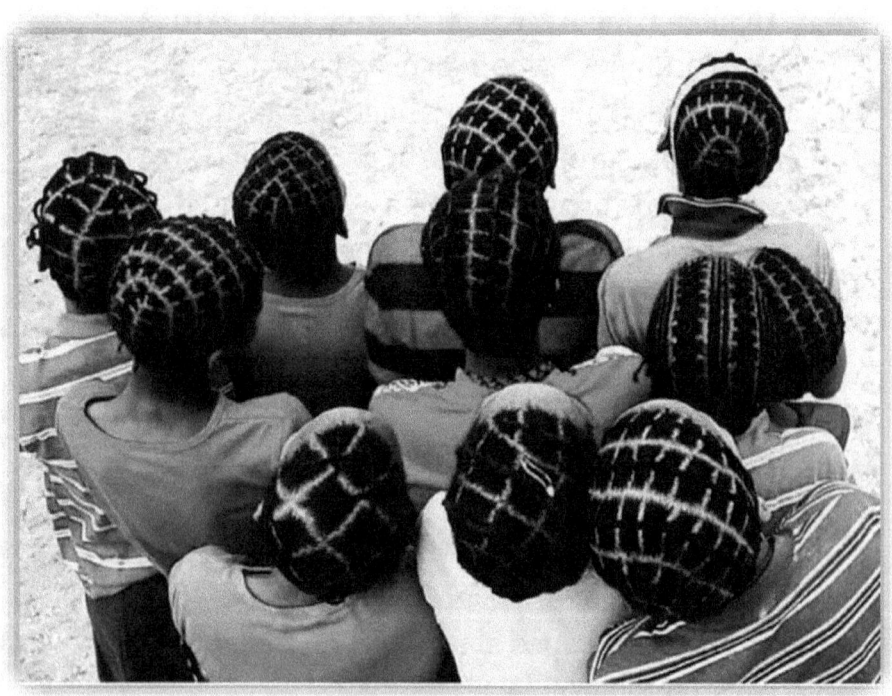

Cornrows

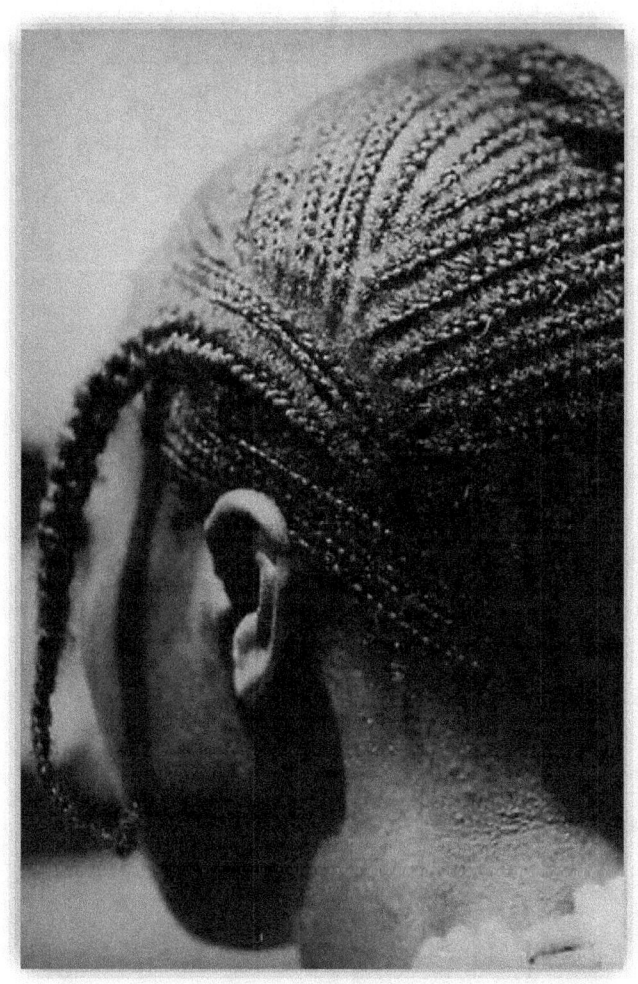

Cornrows

The enslavement of Africans came the oppression of Black hair. From the arrival in the Americas to plantation life and beyond, history shows a common trend of repressing African hair. On the plantation, the men who worked the fields wore their heads shaved, while women were expected to cover their hair with rough, coarse fabric because Europeans considered it unattractive and offensive. Enslaved Africans who worked closer to the plantation "masters" wore hairstyles that emulated the dominant trends of the times, such as wigs in the 18th century. Africans on the plantations either had to emulate white people or cover their heads in an effort not to offend Whites. This concept carries into our present society in a somewhat more nuanced manner.

CHAPTER EIGHT

Benefactors of Black Hair

Benefactors of Black Hair

The late 1800s gave birth to a Black hair care boom. Two historical pioneers of the Black hair care industry are Madame C.J. Walker and Anna Turbo Malone, who created their hair straightening line in the late 1800s and launched their company in the early 1900s. Malone and Walker created lines that were specific to the hair needs of Black women. Malone urged women of African descent to see themselves as African first.

The glaring contradiction lies within the fact that while urging African women to be themselves, Malone created a product meant to straighten their natural, tightly coiled hair. This contradiction continues to be part of the struggle of many Black women because the ideals are so deeply seated and have circulated from one generation to the next.

Although Malone created a hair care line specific to the needs of African American women before Walker, history has been more favorable to Madame C.J. Walker whose popularity greatly exceeds that of Malone's.

Madame CJ Walker wanted Blacks to feel pampered and cared for and be allowed to experience beauty rituals, something Africans had rarely, if ever, experienced after being captured and brought to the Americas.

Johnson, Tabora A., and Teiahsha Bankhead. "Hair It Is: Examining the Experiences of Black Women with Natural Hair." Open Journal of Social Sciences, vol. 02, no. 01, 2014, pp. 86–100. https://doi.org/10.4236/jss.2014.21010.

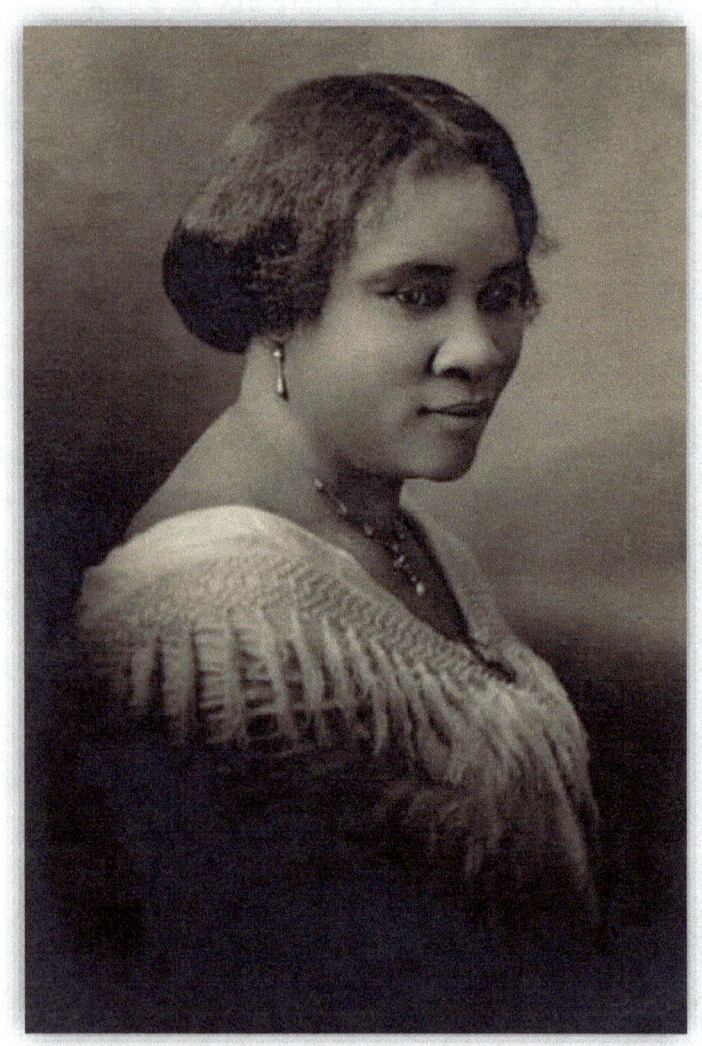

Madam CJ Walker

Madam CJ Walker's name at birth was Sarah Breedlove. She was born December 23, 1867, in Delta, Louisiana. Her parents had six children. Sarah was their fifth child. Slavery had ended two years before Sarah Breedlove was born, and the Breedlove family was very poor, just like most newly freed black families living in the South were after the Civil War.

Families worked all day on farms. As soon as children were six or seven years old, they had to help on the farm too. There was always a lot of hard work to do; plowing, planting, weeding, and taking care of animals. Sarah also had to help out with household chores and laundry. Most black children went to school for two to five months because they were needed on the farm. However, Sarah did not have a chance to go to school when she was a child.

Oluonye, Mary N. Madam C.J. Walker: Inventor, Entrepreneur, Millionaire. CreateSpace Independent Publishing, 2014.

By the time Sarah was seven years old, both of her parents were dead. It was now up to her younger sister, Louvenia, to take care of Sarah and her younger brother Solomon. It was a struggle, and life was very difficult.

Vicksburg, Mississippi, was a short trip across the Mississippi River from Delta, Louisiana, where Sarah lived. Although people traveled easily between Delta and Vicksburg, many felt that there were more opportunities in Vicksburg. When Sarah was ten, they moved to Vicksburg, Mississippi, where their older brother was already living. When they arrived in Vicksburg, however, they found that there were not many jobs available. Louvenia eventually found a job washing clothes, and Sarah helped her. But, when Louvenia got married, things took a turn for the worse for Sarah. She disliked the man her sister married. He was often angry and mean. Sarah desperately wanted to get away. So, when Moses McWilliams asked Sarah to marry him, she said yes. She was only fourteen years old.

Oluonye, Mary N. Madam C.J. Walker: Inventor, Entrepreneur, Millionaire. CreateSpace Independent Publishing, 2014.

Three years later, Sarah gave birth to a baby girl. They named her Lelia. Unfortunately, two years later, Sarah's husband died, and suddenly, at the age of twenty, Sarah was a widow with a young child and very little money.

Sarah moved north to St. Louis, where a few of her brothers had taken up as barbers, themselves having left the Delta as "escaping violence some years before. Sarah lived on $1.50 a day as a laundress and cook, and she struggled to send her daughter Lelia to school. Later, Sarah joined the A.M.E. church, where she networked with others, including those in the National Association of Colored Women.

In 1894, Sarah tried marrying again, but her second husband, John Davis, was less than reliable, and he was unfaithful. At 35, her life remained anything but certain. "I was at my tubs one morning with a heavy wash before me," she later told the New York Times. "As I bent over the washboard and looked at my arms buried in soapsuds, I said to myself: 'What are you going to do when you grow old, and your back gets stiff? Who is going to take care of your little girl?'

Adding to Sarah's woes was the fact that she was losing her hair. As her great-granddaughter A'Lelia Bundles explains in an essay she posted on America.gov's Archive: "During the early 1900s, when most Americans lacked indoor plumbing and electricity, bathing was a luxury. As a result, Sarah and many other women were going bald because they washed their hair so infrequently, leaving it vulnerable to environmental hazards such as pollution, bacteria, and lice."

In the lead-up to the 1904 World's Fair in St. Louis, Sarah's personal and professional fortune began to turn when she discovered the "The Great Wonderful Hair Grower" of Annie Turnbo (later Malone), an Illinois native with a background in chemistry who'd relocated her hair-straightening business to St. Louis. It more than worked, and within a year, Sarah went from using Turnbo's products to selling them as a local agent. Perhaps not coincidentally, around the same time, she began dating Charles Joseph ("C.J.") Walker, a savvy salesman for the St. Louis Clarion.

While still a Turnbo agent, Sarah stepped out of her boss' shadow in 1905 by relocating to Denver, where her sister-in-law's family resided (apparently, she'd heard black women's hair suffered in the Rocky Mountains' high but dry air). C.J. soon followed, and in 1906 the two made it official — marriage No. 3 and a new business start — with Sarah officially changing her name to "Madam C.J. Walker."

Around the same time, she awoke from a dream in which, in her words: "A big black man appeared to me and told me what to mix up for my hair. Some of the remedies were grown in Africa, but I sent for it, put it on my scalp, and in a few weeks, my hair was coming in faster than it had ever fallen out." It was to be called "Madam Walker's Wonderful Hair Grower." Her initial investment: $1.25.

As I started thinking to myself, could that one ingredient from Africa, Madam CJ Walker's, mixed in her scalp ointment be from the chebe plant that grows in a few countries in West Africa? We should know by now that the Basara women in Chad would rub the chebe powder through sections of their hair, which grew their hair to reach to their backsides.

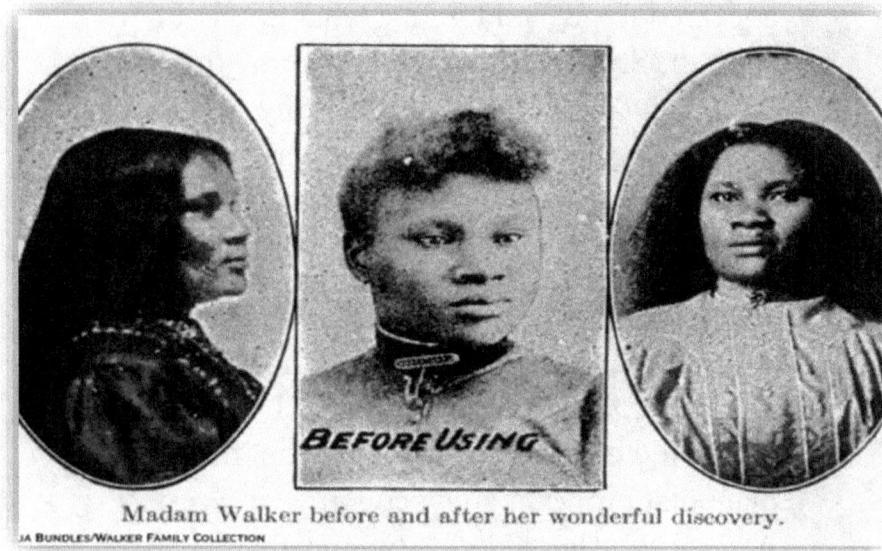

Madam Walker before and after her wonderful discovery.

JA BUNDLES/WALKER FAMILY COLLECTION

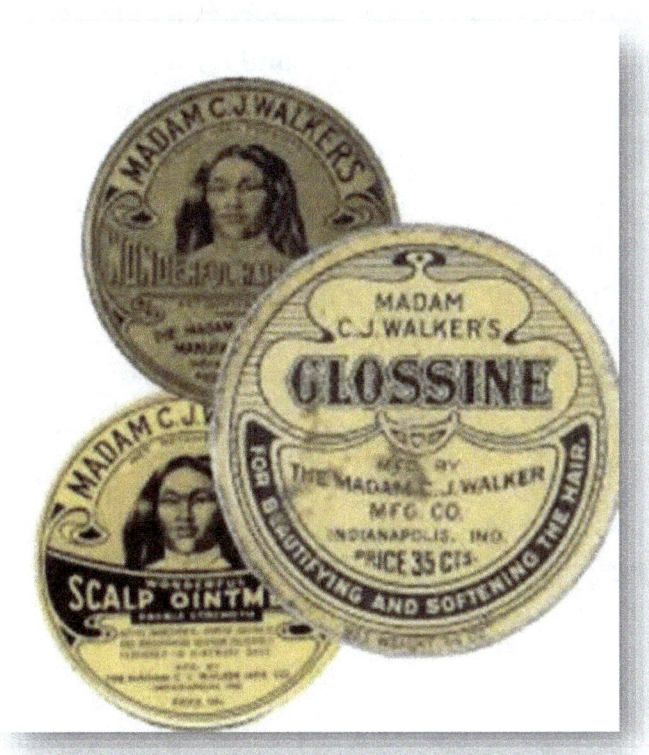

Madam C.J. Walker was very successful; She had her own Walker Manufacturing Company, which was big for a black woman in 1910. Walker Manufacturing Company, headquartered, was a state-of-the-art factory and school in Indianapolis and a major distribution hub. Madam C.J. Walker was a pillar in the black community, providing jobs for thousands of people. Her Walker Agents expanded a number of hair-culture colleges she founded or set up through already established black institutions. There was a whole "Walker System" for them to learn, from vegetable shampoos to cold creams, witch hazel, diets, and those controversial hot combs. Sarah Breedlove (Madam C.J. Walker) was definitely Benefactors of Black Hair.

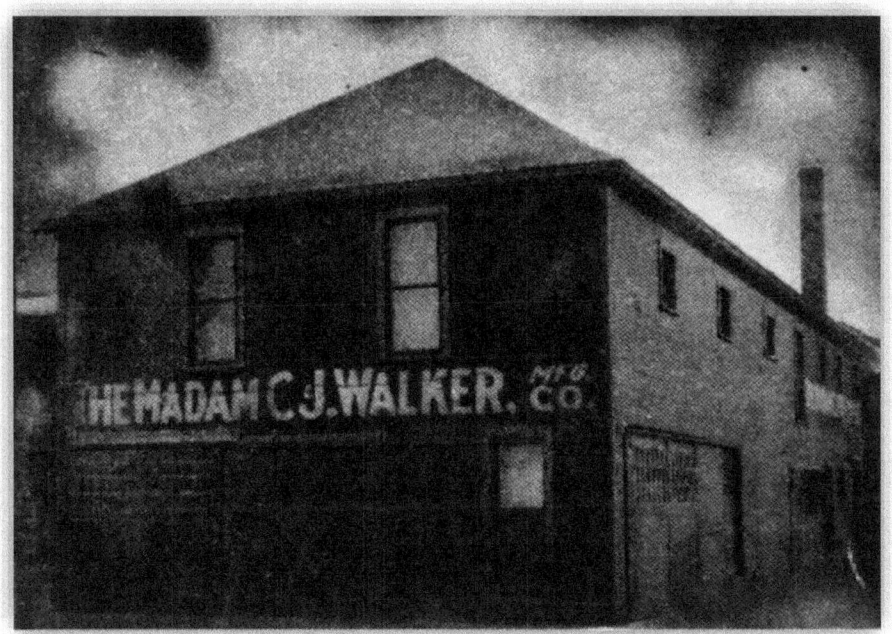

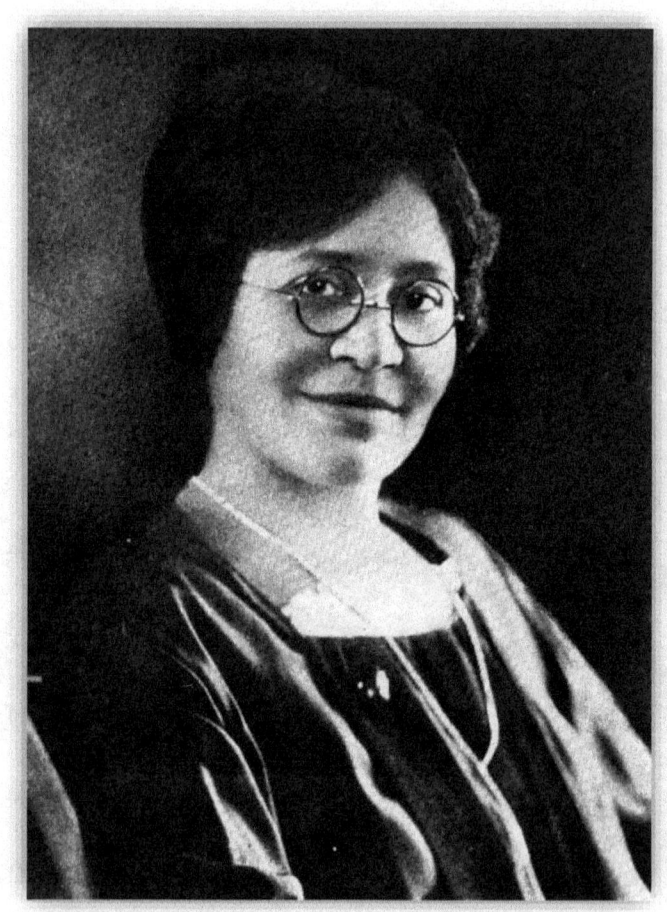

Annie Turnbo Malone

Annie was born in Metropolis, Illinois, to former Kidnap Victims. She was the tenth of eleven children born to Robert Turnbo, a poor farmer, and Isabella Cook Turnbo. Because her parents died when she was young, Annie was raised by her older sister in nearby Peoria, Illinois. She was a sickly child and missed a lot of school, resulting in her having to withdraw before completing high school. While she was coming of age, the popular style among Black women was a "straight hair" look.

Quintana, contributed by: Maria. "Annie Turnbo Malone (1869-1957) 2 June 2020, https://www.blackpast.org/african-american-history/annie-turnbo-malone-1869-1957/.

Black women were starting to turn their backs on the braided cornrow styles they'd associated with the fields of slavery and began to embrace a look that, for them, meant freedom and progression toward equality in America.

While in Peoria, Annie Malone took an early interest in hair textures. In the 1890s, being a lover of styling hair, Annie began to envision a way of straightening hair without having to use the methods of old, which included using soap, goose fat, heavy oils, butter and bacon grease, or the carding combs of sheep. She'd also witnessed methods of hair straightening, which employed lye, sometimes mixed with potatoes but were turned off by the procedure because it often resulted in damaged scalps and broken hair follicles.

Coupled with the influence of her aunt, an herbal doctor, and her knowledge of Chemistry, Annie Turnbo developed a chemical that could be used to straighten hair without causing damage to the hair or scalp. By the time she was in her late 20's, Turnbo had developed a straightening solution that would grant her entry into the annuals of hair care history.

Peter C. Zeppieri, "'For the Good of the Race:' A Case Study in Black Entrepreneurship, 1890-1940" (Thesis, De Paul University, 1993).

By the beginning of the 1900s, Annie Malone began revolutionizing hair care methods for all African Americans. Armed with this revolutionary formula and a product she called "The Great Wonderful Hair Grower," Annie moved to St. Louis in 1902. She hired some assistants and began selling her products door-to-door. Word of her products and teaching method spread like wildfire, and soon, her products and her "Poro Method" of styling hair were a success.

Peter C. Zeppieri, "'For the Good of the Race:' A Case Study in Black Entrepreneurship, 1890-1940" (Thesis, De Paul University, 1993).

Okay, now you see the word Poro; this word is connected to West Africa. The Poro Secret Society. The Poro can be found in many West African countries, including **Liberia**, **Sierra Leone**, **Ivory Coast**, and **Guinea**. The Poro society was part of the culture introduced by the Mande people, migrants to the region as early as 1000 AD, and can sometimes be referred to as the hunting society. Only men are admitted to its rank, but the women's secret society was called the Sande Society.

Among the Mende and the peoples associated with them in Sierra Leone and Liberia, the sanctions on behavior in nearly every sphere of the common life derive largely from secret societies. These societies are, principally, the Poro, the men's society, concerned primarily with the initiation of young boys; the Sande, concerned with women's affairs in nearly every aspect.

Annie Malone had the word Poro all over her skin and hair care products. She had Poro Agents, and a college called Poro college in St. Louis. Annie college in 1926 employed 175 people.

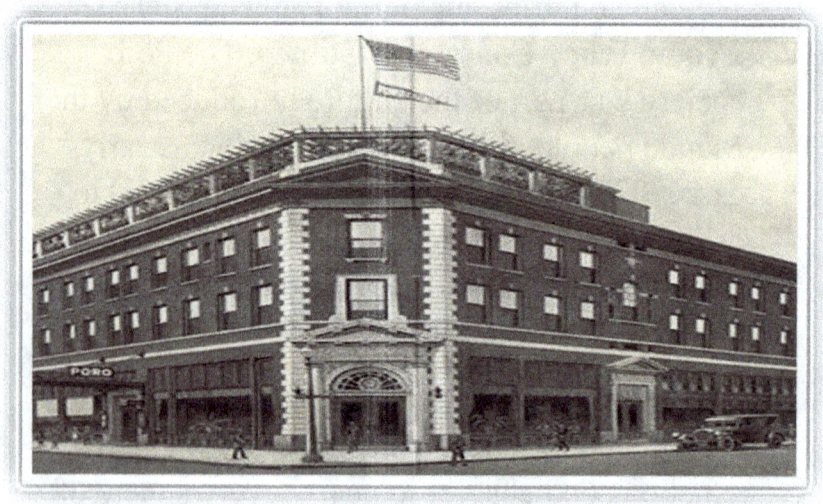

Poro College

The college was the first educational institution in the United States dedicated to studying and teaching black cosmetology. Its curriculum included instructions to train students on personal style to present themselves at work, walking, talking, an, style of dress designed to maintain a solid public persona.

Annie Malone: First African American Millionairess (Educator, Entrepreneur & Philanthropist) -- Courtesy of the Freeman Institute -- Www.porocollege.com, https://freemaninstitute.com/poro.htm.

Annie Malone Franchised her outlets in North and South America, Africa, and the Philippines and employed some 75,000 women. Malone had become a wealthy woman. The Philadelphia Tribune reported that in 1923 Annie Malone paid the highest income tax of any African American in the country. For instance, her 1924 income tax payment totaled nearly $40,000. However, despite her wealth, Malone lived conservatively and gave away much of her fortune to help other African Americans. She is one of America's first major black philanthropists.

Annie Malone: First African American Millionairess (Educator, Entrepreneur & Philanthropist) -- Courtesy of the Freeman Institute -- Www.porocollege.com, https://freemaninstitute.com/poro.htm.

A $25,000 donation from Malone helped build the St. Louis Colored YWCA. From 1919 to 1943, Malone served as board president of the St. Louis Colored Orphan's Home. During this time, she raised most of the orphanage's construction costs. She had donated the first $10,000 to build the orphanage's new building in 1919. With her help, in 1922, it bought a facility at 2612 Annie Malone Drive (formally Goode Ave.) It continues to serve the historic Ville neighborhood. Upgraded and expanded, the facility was renamed in her honor as the Annie Malone Children and Family Service Center in 1946.

Just like Madam C.J. Walker, Annie Turnbo Malone was a pillar in the black community, providing jobs for thousands of people. She was a true philanthropist, and her philanthropic giving was focused on racial uplift, which meant helping African Americans overcome Jim Crow and achieve full citizenship. She gave money to local, regional, national, and international organizations that were typically founded by or focused on serving African Americans.

We must tip our hats off to Annie Turnbo Malone and Madam C.J. Walker because they started thriving black businesses during the Jim Crow era and the Spanish Flu Pandemic. This is very impressive, and both women employed many African Americans and helped many black organizations. These women were innovators, motivators, visionaries, and a blessing to so many communities.

CHAPTER NINE

The Bold and Courageous Melba Tolliver

The Bold and Courageous Melba Tolliver

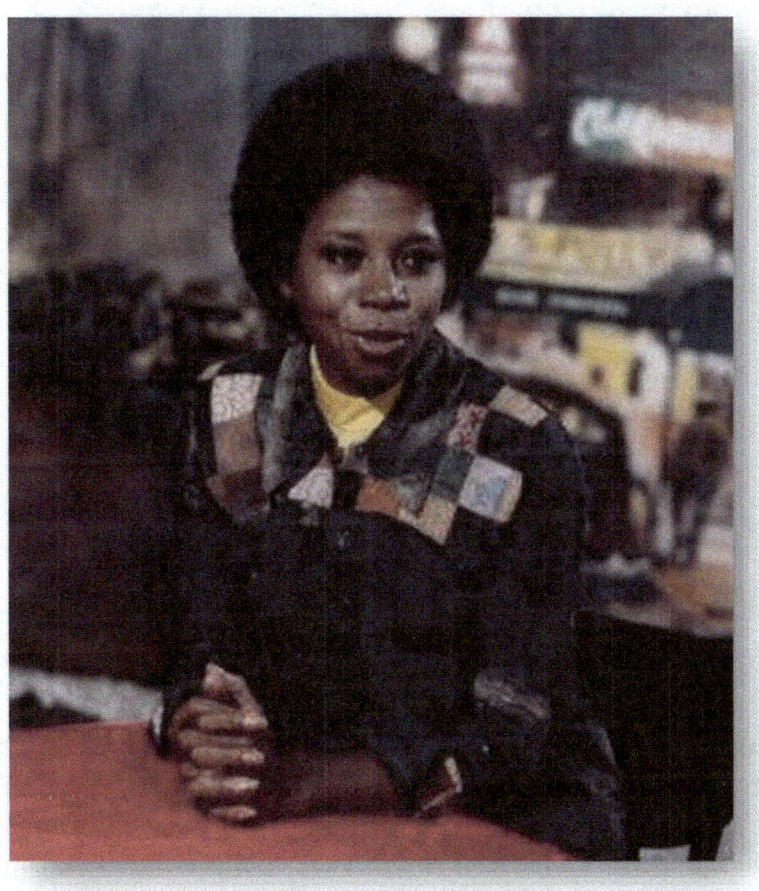

I read an article early this year dealing with hair and ran across Melba Tolliver in an article. The article was very brief about Mrs. Melba Tolliver, and I want to know more about this woman who took a stand when her job wanted her to wear a wig or cover her beautiful afro hair with a scarf to cover the White House wedding of the President Richard Nixon's daughter Tricia Nixon in 1971. Melba Tolliver's job also wanted her to straighten her hair, and she refused to mess up such a perfect and beautiful afro. I will talk more about Melba Tolliver in a few, but first, I want to talk about the resistance movement that started spreading everywhere.

Hair as resistance

By the 50s and 60s, Black hairstyles became an intrinsic part of major Black liberation movements. African Americans had grown frustrated with both the racism they were facing in society and the futility of their own efforts to try and "fit in" just to survive.

"Eventually, enough Black people said this isn't working; it doesn't matter what we do, we're still killed, disrespected, and not allowed to move forward.

And during this time, the afro arose as one of the major symbols of Black agitation in America. "It wasn't about a style. It was a form of protest to say, I am not going to straighten my hair anymore," according to Tharps. "So, the Black afros that we associate with people like Angela Davis, or the Black Panthers of the civil rights movement really became a symbol of resistance."

Tharps, Lori L., and Ayana D. Byrd. Hair Story: Untangling the Roots of Black Hair. St. Martin's, 2002.

The 1960s Black Power Movement was growing, and some Black women and men resisted straightening their hair to reject European beauty standards. Instead, they showed off their naturally textured hair, embracing a "Black is beautiful" mantra. Political activist and scholar. In the 70s, Angela Davis was another powerful sister too, and maybe one day in the future, I can write more about her, but this chapter is about Melba Tolliver. On the Next Page is a photo of Angela Davis, a political activist, and scholar, wearing her beautiful Afro hair that became a symbol of resisting against white oppression.

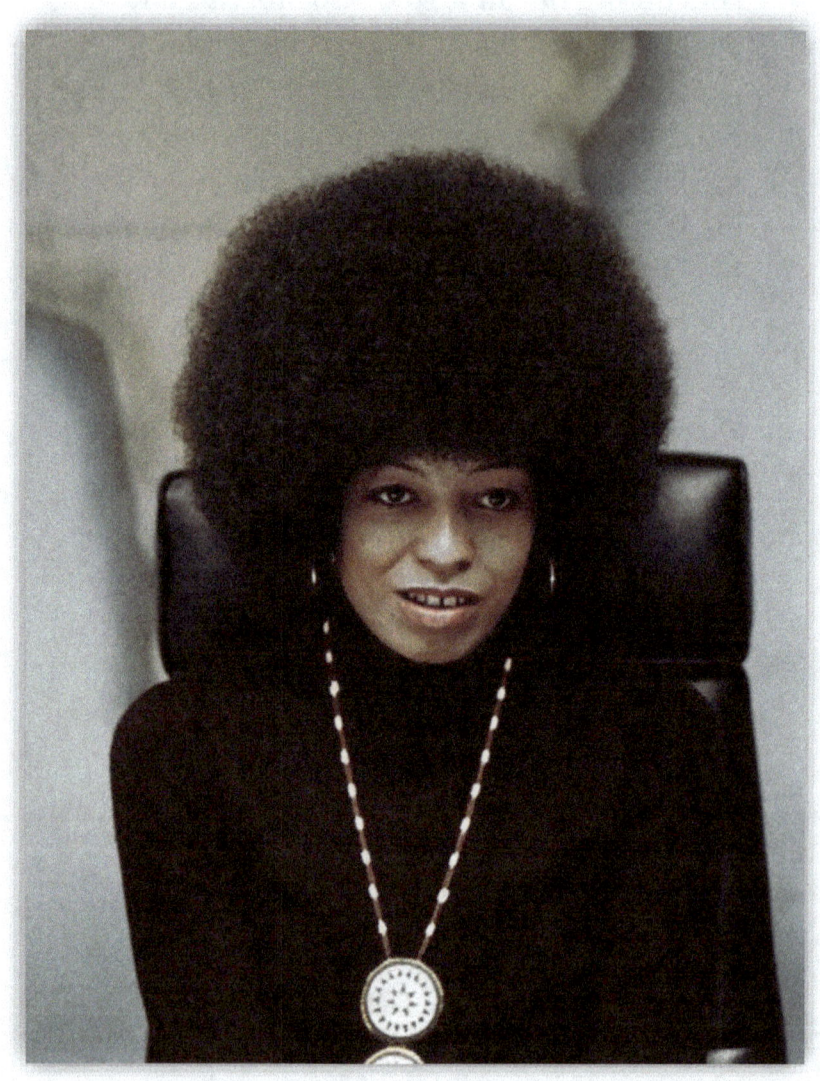

Angela Davis

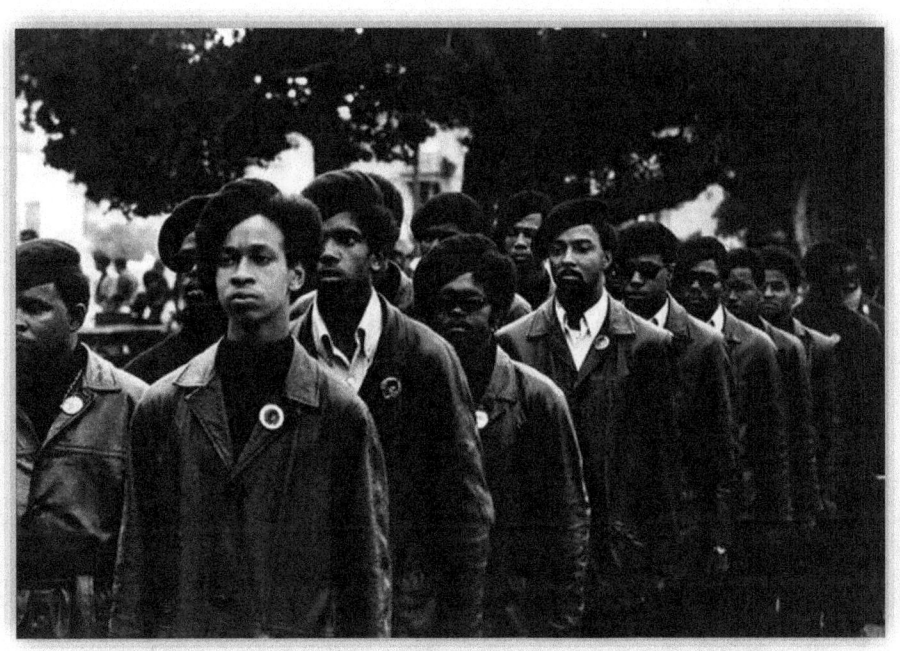

Black Panthers wearing black berets on their Afro's

By the 1970s, advertisements targeted at straightening Black hair expanded to include ads for products to create the perfect Afro.

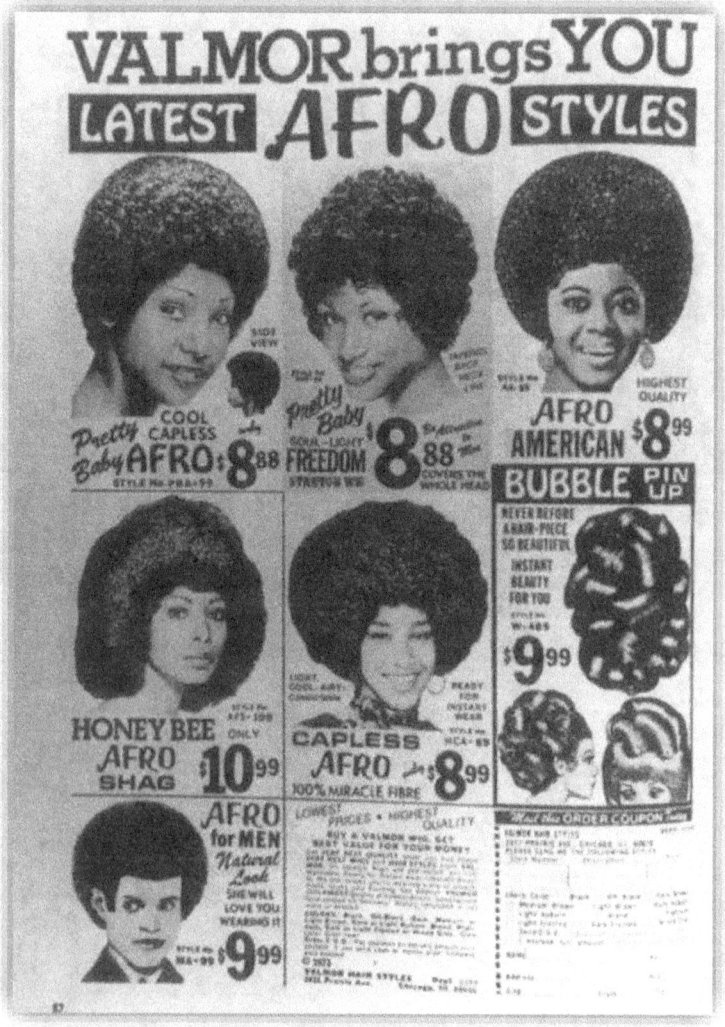

Back to the bold and courageous Melba Tolliver, who was born December 7, 1939, in Rome, Georgia. She worked as a registered nurse and later became a secretary at ABC in November 1966. Strikes by the American Federation of Television and Radio Artists in April 1967 and by the National Association of Broadcast Employees and Technicians in September led to short stints where Tolliver filled in for Marlene Sanders.

Dallos, Robert E. (September 26, 1967). "TV Strike, Burden for Some, Gives Others the Big Chance." The New York Times.

In the summer of 1971, Melba Tolliver's hairdo caused much concern among executives at WABC television. This was the day before she was supposed to cover the White House wedding of President Richard Nixon's daughter Tricia Nixon. Previously Melba had been wearing her hair straight, but she changed it to her natural hair, and the news director told her she could not appear live in the studio unless she changed her hair to how it used to look. They told Melba she looked less attractive and less feminine. We all know the beauty standard is straight hair, and natural hair is ugly, disgusting, and unattractive. Sadly, it is still kind of that way in the 21st century, but I see a resurgence of women returning to their natural hair and getting away from the European standard.

After the bold and courageous Melba Tolliver was asked to straighten her hair, she refused, and then she was told she could not sit in the studio behind the long table with Grimsby and Beutel to do a wrap-up of the weekend wedding.

During an interview with New Your Times, Melba Tolliver recalled they didn't want her to appear on the tape either, but it couldn't be avoided. She further explains she wasn't about to go back to straightening her hair and she probably wouldn't be at WABC today if it hadn't been for an article in The New York Post letting people know what was going on.

Campbell, Barbara. "Melba? She's the Toast of the Town." The New York Times, The New York Times, 18 Feb. 1973, https://www.nytimes.com/1973/02/18/archives/melba-shes-the-toast-of-the-town-melba-tolliver.html.

Melba continues in the interview; when all of that happened with my hair, there wouldn't have been a problem if there had been a black in authority at the station. That's why it's important to have blacks behind the scenes, not just someone in front of the camera who doesn't murder the English language. Those executives had no idea what it meant to me to wear my hair natural or what a stigma it had been for black women in the past to have kinky hair. They interpret news about blacks and minorities through their own perspective as if no other perspective exists.

Campbell, Barbara. "Melba? She's the Toast of the Town." The New York Times, The New York Times, 18 Feb. 1973, https://www.nytimes.com/1973/02/18/archives/melba-shes-the-toast-of-the-town-melba-tolliver.html

Melba Tolliver was the first Black woman to appear on camera on a national news broadcast with her hair in a natural style. She became a new kind of celebrity television superstar reporter. Melba was asked for her autograph while covering a funeral or when she was cheered as she arrived to cover white demonstrators protesting the construction of low-income housing in Forest Hills. Her concern, she says, is with accomplishment beyond being a celebrity. Melba Tolliver was a very smart lady and accomplished a lot in her life, and we should continue to give this bold and courageous black woman her flowers.

CHAPTER TEN

Do African Americans Overspend When it Comes to Our Hair & Beauty

Do African Americans Overspend When it Comes to Our Hair & Beauty

400 years of slavery, a clear health and beauty consciousness was created through Black hair maintenance. Just reading and looking at some of the stats, we are still damaged by the effects of slavery. By now, we know our Ancestor's image was attacked almost daily on those plantations. After slavery, the standard of beauty was lighter skin and straight hair. Those who passed the brown paper bag test were afforded some opportunities. The men and the women begin to straighten their hair with all types of gung. In the twenty-first century, black beauty standards have not really changed. We have made some progress. I am starting to notice where we are now, and that is embracing our natural hair and avoiding putting dangerous chemicals into our hair. We still haven't completely erased the words nappy, good and bad hair out of our vocabulary, and I hope one day we can.

The big hair and beauty industries we (The African Americans) do not own, and coming out of slavery, we have made those industries rich by putting those relaxers with dangerous chemicals into our hair so our hair wouldn't be so call nappy to meet that standard of what we thought was beauty. As I said, we have made progress, but we have created problems where we are the biggest consumer of hair care products.

How much do we spend?

I read a very interesting article by Janine Griffiths called 70+ Key Black Hair Industry Statistics & Facts in 2022, and she states right off the rip in the article that in the US alone, black consumers spend over $1T each year, and a significant amount of that spending goes toward hair care products. According to some estimates, black consumers spend $473M on hair products annually. When I saw that and was like, wow, I am in the wrong business. Ethnic hair and beauty brands market their products toward black consumers, so let's look at how much the black hair industry is worth.

Personal care and beauty, which includes hair care, is a $518B industry in 2021, according to statista.com. a lot of data in this chapter will come from the article 70+ Key Black Hair Industry Statistics & Facts in 2022 and

statista.com, which statista.com has been the
market leader in providing reliable business
data. Now, how much revenue do black hair
brands contribute to the overall hair care
market? Here is what the research revealed:

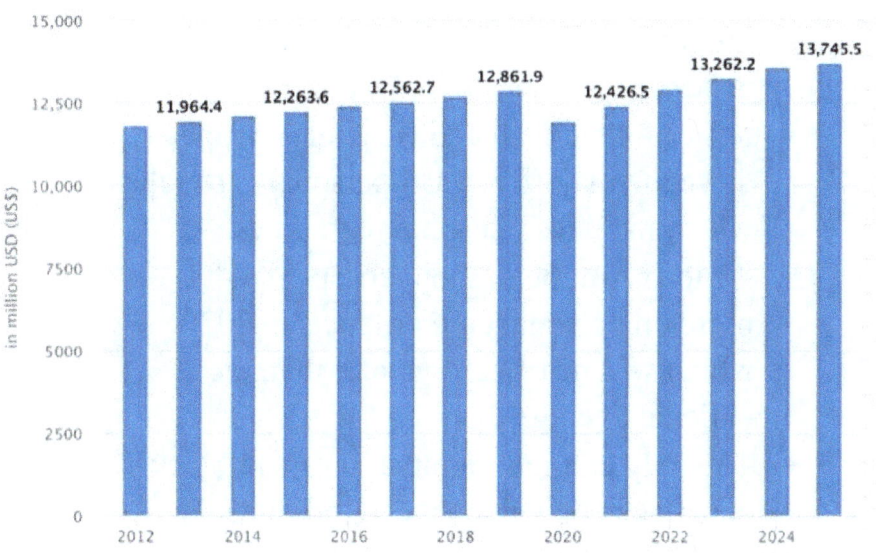

- In the US, the personal care industry, including hair care products, generates $98B in annual sales.
- Each year, black women spend billions of dollars on beauty and personal care products.
- Black women spend 9x more on ethnic hair products than non-black consumers of both genders.
- African American and Hispanic shoppers drive the majority of US personal care sales, which includes black hair care sales.
- African American shoppers spent 5.4% more on personal care products in 2020, which was nearly 2% greater than the national average.
- The only ethnic group that outspent black consumers on personal care products in 2020 were Latin American consumers, spending 2.6% more than the national average.

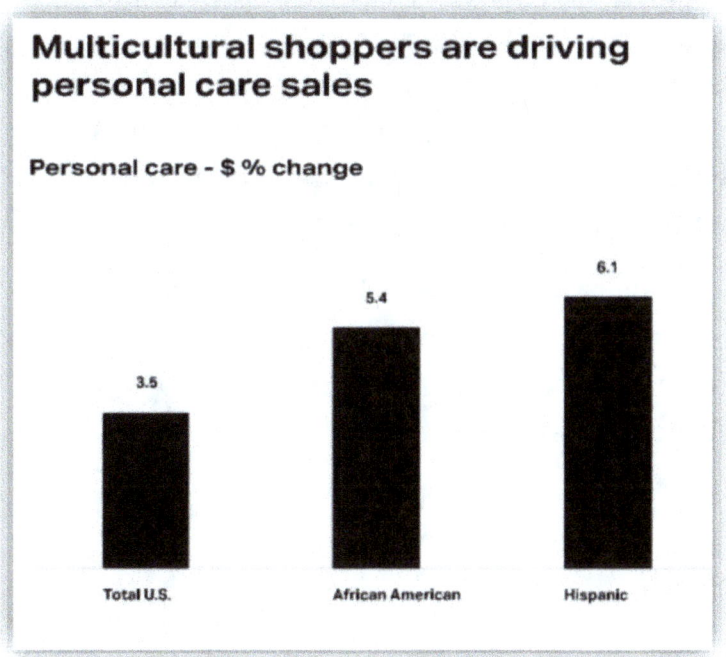

- Black American women who prefer natural hair products are the typical hair care market consumers.
- Experts estimate that the black hair market in the UK is worth £88M or over $120M.

  "Hair Care - United States: Statista Market Forecast." Statista, https://www.statista.com/outlook/cmo/beauty-personal-care/personal-care/hair-care/united-states#revenue.

It's a well-known fact that black consumers punch well above their weight class when it comes to personal care spending. In the US, black consumers are 14% of the population but make up a disproportionate percentage of spending on hair and beauty products. Keep reading to learn more about the power of black dollars.

Black dollars make up 85.7% of the ethnic hair & beauty market. Black consumers spent $54.4M on ethnic hair & beauty products out of $63.5M in total spending on this category.

Black men contribute 21.0% of spending on toiletries, spending $62M out of a total of $308.3M.

Personal soap & bath products are another category where black people spend disproportionately to their US population, spending $573.6M. That's 18.9% of the total $3.04B market.

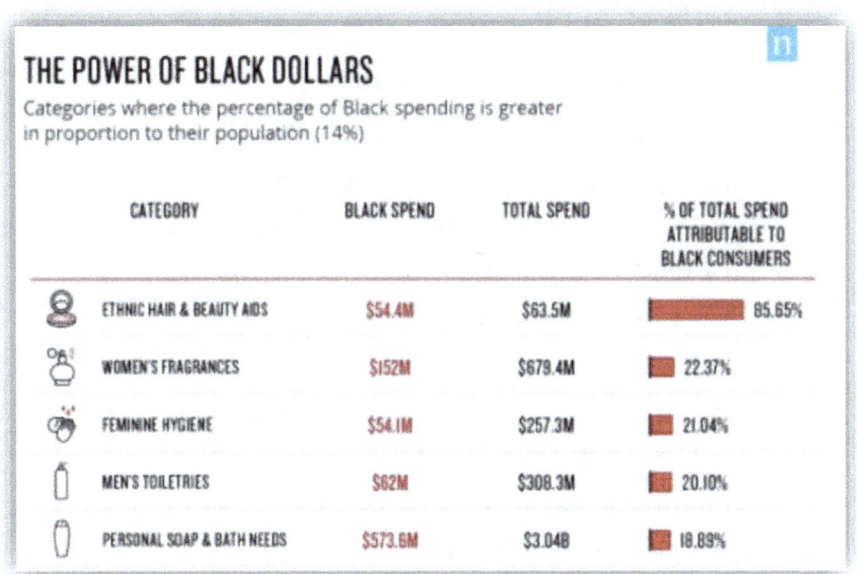

THE POWER OF BLACK DOLLARS

Categories where the percentage of Black spending is greater in proportion to their population (14%)

CATEGORY	BLACK SPEND	TOTAL SPEND	% OF TOTAL SPEND ATTRIBUTABLE TO BLACK CONSUMERS
ETHNIC HAIR & BEAUTY AIDS	$54.4M	$63.5M	85.65%
WOMEN'S FRAGRANCES	$152M	$679.4M	22.37%
FEMININE HYGIENE	$54.1M	$257.3M	21.04%
MEN'S TOILETRIES	$62M	$308.3M	20.10%
PERSONAL SOAP & BATH NEEDS	$573.6M	$3.04B	18.89%

- income on hair care and beauty products.
- 81% of black people say that hair and beauty products advertised through black media channels are more relevant to their needs.
- 43% of black spending power can be attributed to womcn.

> Griffiths, Janine, et al. "Key Black Hair Industry Statistics & Facts in 2022." AfroLovely, 27 Sept. 2022, https://afrolovely.com/black-hair-industry-statistics/.

- In 2018, black consumers spent $473M on hair products, which is 11.3% of sales for the $4.2B hair care industry.
- Black consumers in the US spend disproportionately on styling products. Styling products are only 16% of the total hair care market, but black people spend 35% of their hair care budgets on styling products.
- 51% of black consumers use hair styling products, while only 34% of non-black consumers use styling products.
- Black styling product spending surpassed $1.4B in 2020.
- Experts project that styling product spending among black consumers will decline from 2021 to 2025.
- During the COVID-19 pandemic, black consumers were 2.4 times more likely than the average consumer to purchase hair treatments.
- Black women spend $1.1B annually on wigs, weaves, and extensions.
- From 2016 to 2018, black spending on shampoo and conditioner grew 12.2% and 7.3%, respectively.

- Shampoo and conditioner sales have continued to grow among black consumers in 2019 and 2020.
- In 2021, hair color sales grew amongst the black consumer base.
- Studies show that, among black consumers, financial status makes no difference in hair care product purchases.
- Low-income households make up 43.3% of the market for black hair and beauty products. Low-income black consumers also make up 39.1% of hair and beauty spending, which is higher than middle- and high-income spending in this category.
- 41% of black American women say that the COVID-19 pandemic has forced them to change their hair routines, leading to increases in new product category spending.

Griffiths, Janine, et al. "Key Black Hair Industry Statistics & Facts in 2022." AfroLovely, 27 Sept. 2022, https://afrolovely.com/black-hair-industry-statistics/.

I discuss early in this chapter that coming out of slavery, the standard of beauty was lighter skin and straight hair, and we started putting all kinds of gung with dangerous chemicals into our hair. Later in the 60s, in what I call the first natural hair movement, black people began to reclaim their natural hair or texture after decades of hair-based discrimination. The natural hair movement died out as black people entered corporate workspaces in the 1980s.

Over the last few decades, the movement to reclaim natural black hair has re-emerged. Keep reading below to learn about the driving factors of what I call the second natural hair movement today.

- In 2016, perms & relaxers were the most popular hair service provided to black customers. Approximately 65% of services fell into this category.
- Permanent waves & texturizers were the second most common service provided by black hair stylists at around 62% of services provided.
- At 60% of all services, hair dying was the third most common request by black women in 2016.

- Brazilian blowouts, press & curls, and protective hairstyles were the least-requested hair service in 2016, making up 15%, 255%, and 28% of services provided, respectively.
- A study looked at the percentage of black personal care products with toxic ingredients and found that 58% of hair products marketed toward black people contained one or more toxic ingredients.

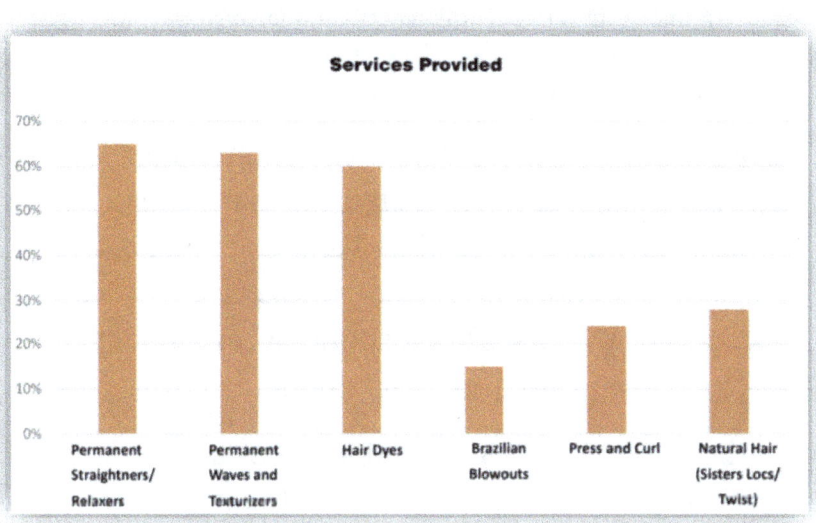

In recent years, the use of these harsh products has declined as Black women seem to favor more natural hairstyles. The market analysis firm Mintel estimates that sales of hair relaxers marketed to Black women dropped nearly 40 percent between 2008 and 2015.

Mintel, Black Consumers, and Haircare – US – August 2015. Available at store.mintel.com/black-consumers-and-haircare-us-august-2015. See also: Mintel, Natural Hair Movement Drives Sales of Styling Products in US Black Haircare Market. Dec. 17, 2015. Available at www.mintel.com/press-centre/beauty-and-personal-care/natural-hair-movement-drives-sales-of-styling-products-in-us-black-haircare-market

Conversely, sales of shampoos, conditioners, and styling products marketed for "natural hair" are increasing. Between 2013 and 2015 alone, sales of "natural" hair styling products increased by about 27 percent, now comprising 35 percent of the Black hair care market.

Although "natural" hair products presumably have fewer toxic ingredients than traditional hair straighteners, many of these products still contain potentially harmful ingredients. Laboratory tests on some products commonly used by Black women, including hair and skin lotions, conditioners, and creams, showed estrogenic or anti-estrogenic activity, meaning that they mimicked the effects of the hormone estrogen. Other studies have found that Black Americans had higher urinary concentrations of parabens, the hormone-disrupting chemicals commonly used as preservatives in personal care products, pharmaceuticals, and foods.

Sharon L. Myers et al., Estrogenic and Anti-Estrogenic Activity of Off-the-Shelf Hair and Skin Care Products. Journal of Exposure Science and Environmental Epidemiology, May 2015. Available at www.ncbi.nlm.nih.gov/pubmed/24849798

The second natural hair care movement came about as we begin to become more aware through us studying and understanding the chemicals that we put into our hair are linked to baldness, growth in the uterus, premature birth, and low infant birth weight, among other things.

The Black Hair and Beauty industries have made billions off us, and is it the effects of the Trans- Atlantic Slave Trade that's, has us going crazy by overdoing it when it comes to beauty. Our spending habits are crazy when it comes to hair and beauty products. We love to look good. When the black man steps out, we got to have the crispy edge up, stylish braids, sheen locs, and clean outfit on. Our shoes got to be right, and if not you, not really clean. When the black woman steps out anywhere, they got to have their hair on fleet, nails, and feet on fleet and a nice and expensive outfit on.

Their nothing wrong with looking good. I am just saying we overdo it, which leads to putting a lot of dollars in the accounts of the owners of these hair and beauty industries. We don't own those industries, so our insecurities about ourselves keep us spending crazy amounts of money with these industries. I'll pose the question again do you all think we are overdoing it when it comes to hair and beauty because of how we were treated in slavery?

Sources

Administrator. "Radical Objects: The Black Fist Afro Comb." History Workshop, 5 Sept. 2022, https://www.historyworkshop.org.uk/radical-objects-the-black-fist-afro-comb/.

Wright, L. (2018). What they don't tell you at the hair salon: It's time for a new conversation about hair. D & C Publishing

"Homo Erectus." The Smithsonian Institution's Human Origins Program, 30 June 2022, https://humanorigins.si.edu/evidence/human-fossils/species/homo-erectus.

Boaz, Noel Thomas, and Russell L. Ciochon. Dragon Bone Hill an Ice-Age Saga of Homo Erectus. Oxford University Press, 2004.

Hair Prehistory., http://thehistoryofthehairsworld.com/hair_prehi story.html.

Byrd, Ayana D., and Lori L. Tharps. Hair Story: Untangling the Roots of Black Hair in America. St. Martin's Griffin, 2002.

Sherrow, Victoria. Encyclopedia Of Hair A Culture History. 2006.

Rolf Gundlach, Matthias Rochholz. Ägyptische Tempel, pp. 304–307 and 310–311.

Lebo Matshego, A History Of African Women's Hairstyles https://african.com/history-african-womens - hairstyles/

Sieber, Roy, and Frank Herreman. "Hair in African Art and Culture." African Arts, vol. 33, no. 3, 2000, https://doi.org/10.2307/3337689.

Sandeen, Del. "7 Myths about Natural Black Hair." Byrdie, Byrdie, 26 Dec. 2021, https://www.byrdie.com/myths-about-natural-black-hair-400343.

Valenti, Lauren. "How the Nomadic Women of Chad Are Keeping the Ancient Hair-Care Ritual of Chébé Alive." Vogue, 8 Mar. 2022, https://www.vogue.com/article/chebe-hair-ritual-chad.

Arsian GG, et al. (2011). An examination of the effect of castor oil packs on constipation in the elderly.ncbi.nlm.nih.gov/pubmed/21168117

Institute of Medicine. Committee on Strategies to Reduce Sodium Intake; Henney, Jane E.; Taylor, Christine Lewis; Boon, Caitlin S. (2010). "4: Preservation and Physical Property Roles of Sodium in Foods"

Bozdogan, Cihangir. "Chebe Powder from Chad for Natural Hair Growth: 4C Natural Afro Hair." Jostylin, https://jostylin.com/chebe-powder-for-natural-hair-growth.

Alfred Thomas (2002). "Fats and Fatty Oils". Ullmann's Encyclopedia of Industrial Chemistry. Weinheim: Wiley-VCH

Mercy, et al. "Shea Butter Origins: Where Does Shea Butter Come from?" Better Shea Butter Shea Butter Origins Where Does Shea Butter Come From Comments, 6 May 2019, https://bettersheabutter.com/where-does-shea-butter-come-from

Botchwey, Adom Tabbey. Ancient African Hair Care Products That Worked Wonders. Face2Face Africa , n.d..

Akorli, Rudith Senam Abla, "Reveal" (2014). Thesis. Rochester Institute of Technology.

Johnson, Tabora A., and Teiahsha Bankhead. "Hair It Is: Examining the Experiences of Black Women with Natural Hair." Open Journal of Social Sciences, vol. 02, no. 01, 2014, pp. 86–100., https://doi.org/10.4236/jss.2014.21010

Griebel, Helen Bradley. The African American Woman's Headwrap: Unwinding the Symbols, http://char.txa.cornell.edu/Griebel.htm.

Clinton, Catherine; Gillespie, Michele (1997-06-26). The Devil's Lane: Sex and Race in the Early South. Oxford University Press. p. 238

Oluonye, Mary N. Madam C.J. Walker: Inventor, Entrepreneur, Millionaire. CreateSpace Independent Publishing, 2014.

Quintana, contributed by: Maria. "Annie Turnbo Malone (1869-1957) 2 June 2020, https://www.blackpast.org/african-american-history/annie-turnbo-malone-1869-1957/.

Peter C. Zeppieri, "'For the Good of the Race:' A Case Study in Black Entrepreneurship, 1890-1940" (Thesis, De Paul University, 1993).

Annie Malone: First African American Millionairess (Educator, Entrepreneur & Philanthropist) -- Courtesy of the Freeman Institute -- Www.porocollege.com, https://freemaninstitute.com/poro.htm.

Tharps, Lori L., and Ayana D. Byrd. Hair Story: Untangling the Roots of Black Hair. St. Martin's, 2002.

Dallos, Robert E. (September 26, 1967). "TV Strike, Burden for Some, Gives Others the Big Chance". The New York Times.

Campbell, Barbara. "Melba? She's the Toast of the Town." The New York Times, The New York Times, 18 Feb. 1973, https://www.nytimes.com/1973/02/18/archives/melba-shes-the-toast-of-the-town-melba-tolliver.html.

Safi, Raheem. The History of Durags. 2022.

"Hair Care - United States: Statista Market Forecast." Statista, https://www.statista.com/outlook/cmo/beauty-personal-care/personal-care/hair-care/united-states#revenue.

Griffiths, Janine, et al. "Key Black Hair Industry Statistics & Facts in 2022." AfroLovely, 27 Sept. 2022, https://afrolovely.com/black-hair-industry-statistics/.

Sharon L. Myers et al., Estrogenic and Anti-Estrogenic Activity of Off-the-Shelf Hair and Skin Care Products. Journal of Exposure Science and Environmental Epidemiology, May 2015. Available at www.ncbi.nlm.nih.gov/pubmed/24849798

Singleton, Saleam. "The History of the Durag and How It Became a Cultural Symbol of Pride." Byrdie, Byrdie, 15 Sept. 2022, https://www.byrdie.com/history-of-durag-4798963.

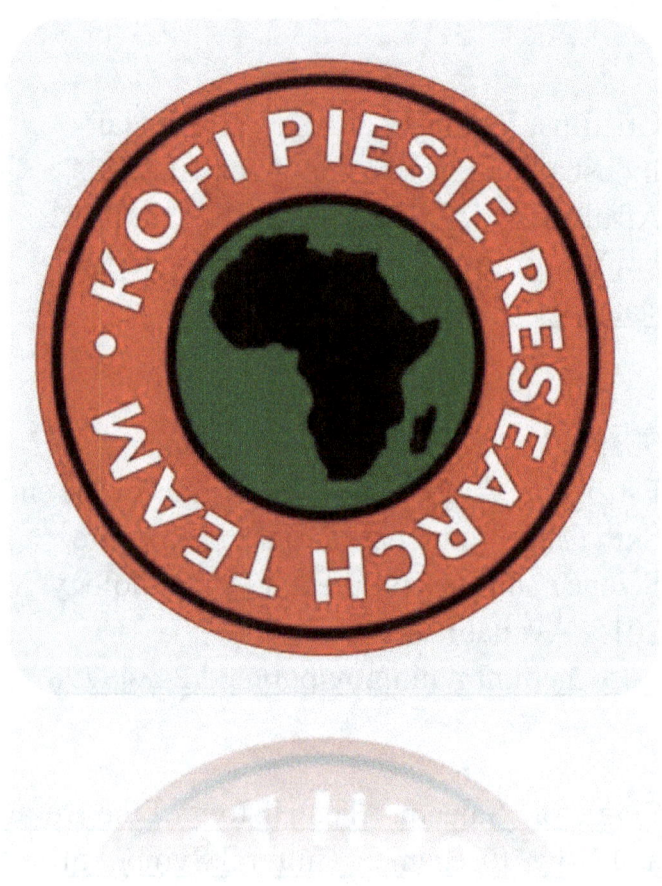

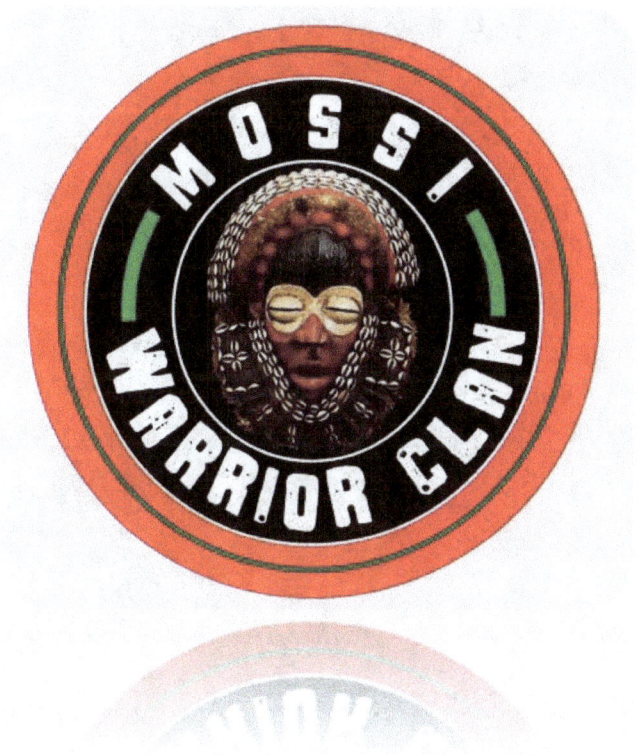

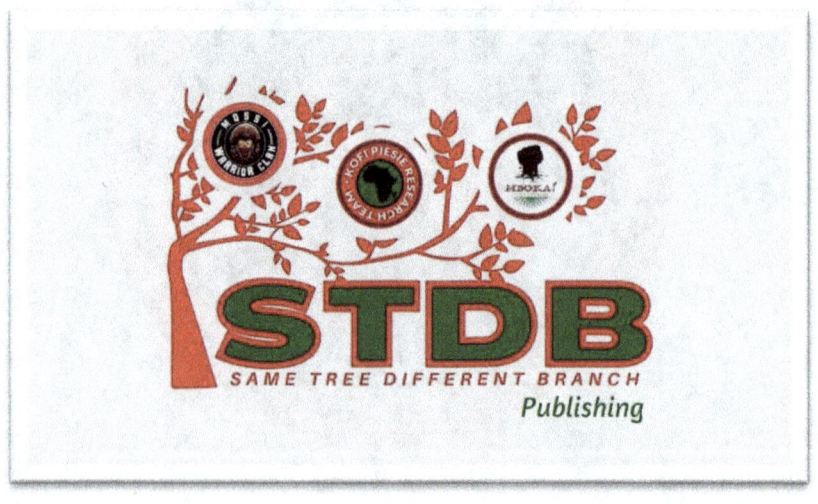